MW00931327

The Mental Game of Football

Playing the Game One Play at a Time

MASTERS OF THE MENTAL GAME SERIES BOOK

This book is being given to

_____

Because I care about you and your success

_____

Brian M. Cain, MS, CMAA
with Daniel C. Nolan

Brian Cain Peak Performance, LLC

www.BrianCain.com

WHAT CHAMPIONS ARE SAYING ABOUT BRIAN CAIN AND *THE MENTAL GAME OF FOOTBALL*

"Cain gives you a system for communicating and teaching more effectively about competitiveness, mental toughness and the skills athletes need to succeed in college football and in life. His program made a huge difference in our 2010 Big South championship season."

David Bennett
Former Head Football Coach
Coastal Carolina University
2010 Big South Champions

"Brian Cain is a big part of our program at Yale. Our coaches and players have benefited tremendously from his ability to give us tools to use to help slow the game down, play one play at a time and give ourselves the best chance for success."

Tony Reno
Head Football Coach
Yale University

"I have worked with Brian Cain and his One Play at a Time System since I was at Washington State, and it has made a HUGE difference in the way I approach the game. It gives our coaches and players something to go to when the game starts to speed up."

Chris Ball
Defensive Coordinator
Arizona State University

"Brian Cain and The Mental Game of Football are trendsetters and game changers. This book will positively impact the way you approach the game."

Tom Perry
Head Football Coach
Colchester High School

"Having a system to play the game one play at a time was a huge difference maker in our success at Midland Lee High School."

James Morton
Head Football Coach
Midland Lee High School
Midland, Texas

"I have worked with Brian Cain for the last 10 years. The cat is out of the bag. He is the best in the country at coaching the mental game of football. If you are not using his system to play one play at a time, you are cheating your players out of peak performance."

Donald Hawes
Bear River High School
Tremonton, Utah

"There are lots of talented high school football players that underachieve. They let their emotions and the competitive fire inside of them get the best of them. They have no way to slow the game down. I was always at a loss as to why people with great talent underachieved. After reading this book, now I know. I wish someone had written this book 20 years ago."

Shawn Flaherty
Head Football Coach
Mt. Greylock Regional High School

"Brian Cain is a winner. We have used many of the strategies and tips in this book and they have made a big difference for us in our abilities to stay locked in on the next 30 Feet of The Road."

Hal Wasson
Head Football Coach
Southlake Carroll High School
Southlake, Texas

If this book has had a positive impact on the way you coach or play football and you would like to have a testimonial featured in future editions of *The Mental Game of Football,* please e-mail your testimonial to admin@briancain.com.

We look forward to hearing how this book has positively affected your game and life. We would also welcome the opportunity of working with you to become a master of the mental game, and to helping you DOMINATE the day, one play at a time.

In Excellence,

Your Mental Conditioning Coach for Football

Brian M. Cain, MS, CMAA

MASTERS OF THE MENTAL GAME SERIES BOOK

The Mental Game of Football

Playing the Game One Play at a Time

MASTERS OF THE MENTAL GAME SERIES BOOK

Brian M. Cain, MS, CMAA
with Daniel C. Nolan

Brian Cain Peak Performance, LLC

Brian M. Cain, MS, CMAA
Mental Conditioning Coach
Peak Performance Publishing
Brian Cain Peak Performance, LLC

The Mental Game of Football:
One Play at a Time

A Masters of the Mental Game Series Book

Printed in the United States of America
Edited by: Mary Lou Schueler
Cover design & manual layout: Brian M. Cain, MS, CMAA
Illustrations: Nicole Ludwig and Greg Pajala
Photography: TBD

Brian M. Cain, MS, CMAA with Daniel C. Nolan
The Mental Game of Football:
One Play at a Time
A Masters of the Mental Game Series Book

ISBN-13: 978-1496192271
ISBN-10: 1496192273

PREFACE

Every play in football has a life and history of its own. In most games there will only be a handful of plays that determine the outcome of that game. As a coach or player, you never know what play will be the one that makes the big difference, so you have to treat them all as if they are going to be that big play.

Playing the game of football one play at a time is what the mental game is all about. Giving yourself the best chance for success on this play in turn gives you the best chance for success on the scoreboard at the end of the game.

This book is an extensive collection of my experiences working as a mental conditioning coach in the game of football and is a body of work that, when put into action, will unlock your potential and take your game to the next level.

This is a book about the process of becoming a person with a program of excellence.

This is a book about becoming a champion so that you can win more championships.

This is a book designed for you to become more so that you can get more out of yourself and others.

This book will provide you with the guiding principles that will give you the best chance for success in football and in life.

The material in this book has worked for real football players and coaches in real college and high school programs around the country. This is not a book on theory; it is a book on APPLICATION!

Whether you are a veteran of mental conditioning and football or just getting started, this book will provide insight and information you can use IMMEDIATELY to start becoming and creating masters of the mental game.

DOMINATE THE DAY!

DEDICATION

This book is dedicated to all of the football players and coaches out there who realize the value of the game and the amazing life lessons you learn through participation.

This book is dedicated to you, the reader, because you are committed to excellence. You have chosen to invest the time it takes to be different, abnormal or uncommon, in order to take your game and life to the next level. You want more, and my mission through this book is to help you establish a process so that you can become more.

By signing your name below, you are dedicating yourself to reading and, more importantly, to applying this book and making the commitment to enjoy the journey to the summit of The Mountain of Excellence.

I _____

(print your name) have been given everything I need to become a person of excellence. I am fully capable of living the life of my dreams and leaving this world and the game of football more than it was when I got here. I am a one-play warrior who lives and competes in the present and chooses to focus on the process over the outcome, and I will stay positive in the face of adversity.

ACKNOWLEDGMENTS

It is with sincere and deep appreciation that I, Brian M. Cain, acknowledge the support and guidance of the following people who helped make this manual possible:

Special thanks to Dr. Ken Ravizza, John T. Allen, Dan Nolan, Bruce Brown, Dr. Rob Gilbert, Ed Agresta, Harvey Dorfman, Shawn & Tim Flaherty, Bob Davis, Chris Ball, Paul Wulff, James Morton, Kevin Ozee, Mark Shaw, David Caputi, Matt & Kyle Bombardier, my father Joe Cain (who throws a mean Nevada, aka post route), Ross Ackley, Debbie & Fred Ackley, and all of my teammates at Mt. Greylock Regional High School and with the Lanesboro Tigers (still the greatest athletic experience of my life), and to the thousands of coaches and athletes who have shared their stories with me on the mental game and have influenced the writing of this book.

It is with sincere and deep appreciation that I, Daniel C. Nolan, acknowledge the support and guidance of the following people who helped make this manual possible:

Special thanks to Bob Davis, Brian Cain, Doug D'Olimpio, Eric Johnson, Aaron Grondin, Ben Bouffard, and my incomparable family – Kate Dale; Maura, John, Tim, Jack and Carolyn Nolan; and Tiffany and Davan Russell.

---

www.briancain.com/football
for BONUS Mental Conditioning Material
& FREE Peak Performance Training Tools

CONTENTS

CHAPTER #4
POSITIVE MENTALITY..87

CHAPTER #5

CHAPTER #6
PERFORMANCE ROUTINES

CHAPTER #9
RELAX & RECOVER
MENTAL IMAGERY 179

FOREWORD

This is a book about excellence - excellence in football, and more importantly, excellence in life. If you have this book in your hands, it is my mission that this book will become "that book" – that book that changed your life.

For me, that book was *Heads-Up Baseball: Playing The Game One Pitch At A Time* by Dr. Ken Ravizza. Reading that book changed my life as a baseball player and as a man. I spent two years with Dr. Ravizza in his graduate school program in sport psychology at Cal State Fullerton. Those years and my four years of high school football playing for John T. Allen were the most influential time period of my life because of the growth, self-discovery and model that these men set for me to follow.

This book contains the principles and lessons I have learned from these two great coaches about mental toughness - the same principles and lessons that I teach in the execution of my mission as a mental conditioning and peak performance coach with the top college and high school programs in the country.

In most ways, this manual is the product of my experiences throughout this great journey and learning process. It represents the accumulation of the knowledge I have gained and wish to impart to those who strive for daily excellence and who want to become more so they can have more.

Being in the dugout during the NCAA College World Series in Omaha; working as a mental conditioning coach with Team USA Baseball and NCAA Champions; cornering Ultimate Fighting Championship World Champions in Main Event bouts in Las Vegas; working with athletes competing for their home country in the Olympic Games; and working with coaches and athletes in Major League Baseball, the National Football League, the National Hockey League and in the National Basketball Association as a mental conditioning coach - these are just a few of the standout moments I have been fortunate to experience in my career. Still, to this day, my greatest memories are from high school football. I hope this book helps coaches and players to get even more out of this great game and the greatest athletic experience available to young people in our country.

I am humbled by the privilege I have to live the life of my dreams, and I move forward in life with an attitude of gratitude. I understand, however, that this privilege is not guaranteed to me, and any success is the result of having had the opportunity to surround myself with successful and selfless people who have shown me the way.

Human growth and development happen through experience - the experience of the events in your life, the teammates you have, the people you meet, the programs you watch, the music you listen to, and the books you read. It is my sincere hope and desire that this book becomes a life-changing experience for you on the greatest field in the world, the football field, and in life.

Compete One Play At A Time!!!

AUTHOR'S NOTE

The intent of the author in writing this book in The Masters of the Mental Game Series was to create a comprehensive mental conditioning manual that could be used by football players and coaches as their blueprint for mental conditioning.

Mental conditioning and peak performance are all about searching within yourself to see what you are made of as a person. When you search within yourself, you learn that all the answers to life's questions and challenges live inside you. As you work your way through this book, you will learn what drives you to embark on this self- transformative journey of self-improvement by continuously reflecting upon your attitudes and actions.

While reading this book, you will recognize the mental adjustments and changes you must make to access all the untapped and limitless potential that resides inside you. Tapping into every ounce of combined mental and physical potential is the art of peak performers, and this book will teach you this art form by coaching you to search from within.

This photo has impacted me since I first saw it in 2002, and it illustratively captures the concept of one's ability to search within oneself. My life's mission is to help you uncover the excellence that lies within you and to coach you to develop the tools necessary to achieve your best in football and in life by taking a look inside.

INTRODUCTION

INTRODUCTION TO
PEAK PERFORMANCE,
MENTAL CONDITIONING AND
THE MENTAL GAME OF FOOTBALL

> "Football may be the best-taught subject in American high schools because it is the only subject that we haven't tried to make easy."
>
> **Dorothy Farnan**
> **English Department Chair**
> **Erasmus Hall HS, Brooklyn, New York**

What is peak performance in football? What does it mean to play your best one play at a time? What is mental conditioning and why is it essential to both understanding and answering those two questions?

This is your mental conditioning program for football. A 10-chapter/10-week off-season training program that will give you the knowledge and techniques to unlock all of your performance potential on the gridiron.

The coaches and athletes I have worked with at national championship-winning college programs; state and national championship-winning high school programs; the Olympic Games; Ultimate Fighting Championship; National Football League; National Hockey League; National Basketball Association; and Major League Baseball have all experienced one thing in common: *As you elevate to higher levels of competition, success becomes less about the physical skills and more about your mental game.*

This truth is essential to acknowledging and appreciating the importance of mental conditioning, and the more you think about it, the more obvious it becomes. At the highest levels of competition, everyone has the physical skills to be successful or else they would not be competing at that level. Talent is simply just not enough. If it were, every 1st round pick in the Major League Baseball Draft would make it to the Major Leagues, but less than half of them ever do.

Thus, on top of developing the physical skills to compete at the highest level, coaches and athletes must devote more time to the development of their mental game that will allow them to perform consistently at their best.

To further emphasize the significance of mastering the mental game, there is a simple two-word sentence to convey the significance of mental conditioning as it relates to football: *Consistency wins*.

> "Discipline breeds consistency and consistency is the father of success."
>
> *Tony DeMeo*
> *College Football Head Coach*

CONSISTENCY IN PLAY TO PLAY

Consistency is the significant difference between the good and the great coaches, players and teams. Those who compete at the highest level on a consistent basis are the legendary and iconic figures in the game like Peyton Manning, Walter Payton, Lawrence Taylor and Jerry Rice.

Super Bowl winning head coach Jon Gruden was amazed at Rice's consistency and work ethic, which he observed firsthand when they were both with the Oakland Raiders.

"I had never seen anything like the work ethic of this thirty-nine-year-old Hall of Famer-in-waiting. He would get our practice scripts, and through every second of the pre-practice stretch, he would have a coach quiz him on the pass routes we were going to run that day. Between every period he would be off to the side, on one knee, concentrating and studying the next grouping of plays we were going to run. He hated making mistakes. He had so much pride in getting every detail right; it was amazing."

Anyone who has the physical prowess necessary to compete has the ability to perform at the highest levels of his ability once in a while, but it is the one-play warrior who stands out among everyone else – the one who brings his best every play and every time he puts the helmet on. That is the guy who will make the biggest impact on his team, in his school, and who will ultimately have the greatest career.

WHAT MAKES THE BEST OF THE BEST

Demanding the best possible performance from your body is a characteristic of all great athletes. However, physical development to your peak potential does not come cheap.

The most competitive athletes invest significant amounts of time and energy into the many grueling hours it takes to train their bodies for performance at the highest levels of football. The off-season workouts of Jerry Rice are something of legend and something that you will research on YouTube and use as motivation if you want to get the most out of your career.

MENTAL CONDITIONING IS ESSENTIAL

The greatest players and teams in football are aware of something that you might not realize: **If you want to be the best of the best, doing the physical training is simply not enough.**

Legendary NFL head coach, owner, and Hall of Famer Paul Brown knew this very well. According to Brown:

"The best teams were first and foremost made up of quality people. He was convinced that with diligence, wisdom and teamwork, an assemblage of average players formulated from high-character individuals could – while working in unison as a close-knit crew – achieve much greater success than a group of all-star individuals who were incapable of functioning in harmony."

Brown and other great champions know that mental conditioning is essential in order to develop a psychological edge over their greatest competitors and give them the confidence to turn it loose and play carefree.

The greatest competitors understand that peak performance occurs only when the body and the mind are working together to maximize their performance potential. Thus, the best of the best know that mental conditioning is as vital to their success as physical conditioning.

THE POWER OF THE MIND

The power of the mind is as miraculous as it is incomprehensible. Studies have continued for years, and we are still miles away from truly understanding the full capabilities of the human brain. Countless examples of the "mind over matter" type of experience have been documented over time.

There are incredible examples of prisoners of war being released and performing amazing physical feats that they had practiced mentally during their detentions.

One such example is of a POW who came out of exile having visualized playing golf every day. By the time he was free and stepped onto a golf course, he lowered his golf game by ten strokes. Upon his release, another POW who practiced mental conditioning became a competent guitarist by teaching himself the guitar through repetitive visualization processes, despite never playing the instrument before.

There are endless miraculous stories similar to these, and it is safe to say that even though neurological function is not as well understood as the physiological, no one is prepared to discount the human mind as the most powerful tool available in the world.

The good news is that even without understanding the scientific intricacies of the human mind, anyone can improve his mental toughness for football with a simple mental conditioning program and by doing simple exercises on a routine basis. You learn best in conditioning yourself to be the toughest mentally just like you do physically - by ***doing a little a lot, not a lot a little.***

MENTAL CONDITIONING FOR FOOTBALL

Mental conditioning for football is the process of developing mental toughness, by which an individual exercises and develops the mental muscles to control his mental state in order to control his behavior.

You must be in control of yourself before you can control your performance on the field - and gaining self-control in the violent, aggressive, combative sport of football is essential to your success.

When divided between the two words, mental relates to the mind, while conditioning means to train oneself to behave in a certain way or to accept certain circumstances that will happen in the game, such as an official missing a call, the other team ripping off a big play or you having to play through pain and discomfort.

Mental conditioning is a process similar to how you would physically condition your body in the weight room. When you lift weights infrequently, you don't get any stronger; but when you lift weights consistently, the timely repetition will make you stronger. Mental toughness is developed the same way, by doing a little a lot.

Mental conditioning gives you the techniques to develop control over the beliefs in your mind. Beliefs (both positive and negative) shape our behavior, create our experiences, and determine our results.

THE POWER OF BELIEFS

Philosophers and spiritual leaders have been preaching the power of beliefs for centuries, while scientists have been conducting research on how the mind works for decades. Football coaches – such as the great Bud Wilkinson of Oklahoma, whose teams won three national championships in the 1950's and won 47 straight games between 1953 and 57 - were among the first in our culture to recognize the practical application of positive affirmation training and the implications of mental conditioning for their performance. Wilkinson once famously said, "You can motivate players better with a kind word than with a whip."

Football coaches like Wilkinson realized that they could dramatically improve their players' confidence, resilience in the face of adversity and their on-field performance reliability by integrating positive confidence conditioning statements and mental imagery into their daily training regimens. Jimmy Johnson, one of only three coaches to have won both the Super Bowl and the national championship, said this:

"Treat a man as he is, and he will remain as he is. Treat him as he could be, and he will become what he should be."

The goal of this book is to give you the tools to develop your mental game, shatter limiting beliefs, develop the confidence and consistency needed to play your best one play at a time, and give yourself the best chance to win on the scoreboard and, more importantly, in life.

CAIN'S COACHING POINT:
The mental conditioning skills you will learn to perform at your best in football will also help you to perform at your best in life when your football playing days are over.
Football really is a gateway to life. The skills coaches teach you on the field will help you to perform in the world.

COACHES' BUILT-IN EXCUSE:
NOT HAVING A MENTAL CONDITIONING SYSTEM

It is an unfortunate reality that most football programs leave mental toughness to chance. Many coaches think that their players will either figure it out or they won't - that their players either have it together between the ears or they do not. Many coaches think players are born mentally tough or mentally weak. This old-school thinking is actually excuse making for not knowing how to train and develop mental toughness in their football players.

These coaches believe there is nothing they as coaches can do to help enhance the athlete's mental toughness other than tough physical conditioning, and yet they will agree that performing at your best when it means the most is as much about the six inches between your ears as it is the six feet below them.

This coaching mentality fails to recognize that developing a strong mental game has just as much, if not more, significant value to performance on the field than developing a strong physical game.

EXCUSE EXTERMINATOR IN YOUR HANDS

Until now, mental toughness training for football has been left to chance. In this book, you will learn the importance of focusing on the *present moment* and will gain a true understanding of what it means to have a *process over outcome* approach, a *positive attitude* and *performance preparation routines*, along with the *discipline* and *dedication* necessary to achieve your football and personal goals, regardless of adversity and the failures you will face.

MENTAL TOUGHNESS IS A SKILL SET

Mental toughness is simply a skill set that can be taught, developed, and continuously improved just like your physical game of football.

Mental conditioning is strength and conditioning for the six inches between your ears that control the six feet below them. Having a mental conditioning system is essential to playing your best when it means the most, *one play at a time*. Mental conditioning will give you a skill set to be successful in football and, more importantly, successful in life.

> "Mental is to physical as 4 is to 1."
>
> *Bobby Knight*
> *College Basketball Head Coach*
> *902 wins, 3 national championships*

THE 90%/10% SHIFT

Whether or not coaches and athletes understand the complete significance of mental conditioning, most coaches and athletes I have worked with will agree that training for football games is 90% physical and 10% mental. They acknowledge that a noticeable shift occurs when kickoff rolls around. In the heat of competition they acknowledge that performance becomes 90% mental and 10% physical. This is called the 90%/10% shift to give athletes and coaches an illustrative taste of how valuable mental conditioning is when it is time to put the helmet and shoulder pads on and line it up.

The reality is that there should be no shift. Mental conditioning should be integrated into physical conditioning and every aspect of preparation. It should be 100% mental and physical conditioning combined, because one is never complete without the other.

This book will give you a system for training your mental game and for unlocking your true gridiron potential. As you read this manual and develop your mental toughness, think about it as going to the gym to do strength and conditioning for your brain instead of your body. This book is your "Mind Gym."

CAIN'S BLUEPRINT FOR EXCELLENCE

I always get the question, "Brian, when you work with the top football programs and professional athletes, what do you teach?"

What I teach them is the same mental conditioning program that you will learn - about exactly how to play your best when it means the most, by teaching you how to:

• Live in the present moment and compete one play at a time.

• Act differently than how you feel and start having good and "bad" days and good "bad" plays.

• Focus on the process over the outcome.

• Identify what you can control and what you cannot.

• Have your own personal and program philosophy and core values for football and life.

• Challenge your limiting beliefs and your perspective.

• Stay positive in the face of adversity - and football is a game of adversity.

• Develop preparation and performance routines for consistent high-level football performance.

• Take responsibility for your performance and life.

• Relax, recover, and gain control of your thoughts, feelings, and emotions before the big play and in life.

• Recognize your signal lights and develop the awareness to win the next play and win the day.

• Release negative thoughts and refocus back to the next play when you get distracted and when adversity hits.

• Move from intelligence and thinking to trusting, action and positive results.

• Use mental imagery to help you prepare and be more confident for your next game and next play.

• Inspire, lead and motivate yourself to make the impossible possible.

• Develop the dedication and self-discipline that you need to power through the grind it takes to succeed.

• Take action steps to make excellence a lifestyle, not an event.

These are the fundamentals of mental toughness and represent the blueprint I use when working with any football coach, player or program to develop personal responsibility in daily excellence (PRIDE).

THE GOAL OF THE BOOK IN YOUR HANDS

The goal of the book in your hands is that you learn how to control your mind so you can successfully direct your body to achieve the level of football and life performance necessary to become a champion.

CAIN'S COACHING POINT:
If you want to win a championship, you must first become a champion. Using the skills taught in this book will make you a champion on the field and in life. Always remember that if you want more wins, you must become more as an individual first so that you deserve more wins.

ONE PLAY/DAY AT A TIME
10-WEEK PRIDE PROGRAM FOR FOOTBALL

This book is written in a 10-week program format for building mental toughness for football, a little a lot each week.

We will focus on two critical principles of success:

1. One play/day at a time

2. PRIDE - Personal Responsibility In Daily Excellence

The PRIDE acronym serves as the backbone of this mental conditioning system for football, reminding you of the significance of making excellence a daily pursuit for which you are personally responsible and accountable.

The outcome goal is that you become a peak performer on the field and in life. Before you can become a peak performer, you must first understand that excellence is a lifestyle, not an event, and is defined as being at your best when it means the most which is every day and every play in football.

CAIN'S COACHING POINT:
Excellence is being at your best when it means the most – every play and every day.

For a football player, being your best when it means the most is every single play. Every single rep in practice. Every single lift in the off-season. If you are a student, it is every single class. As former West

Point head football coach Rich Ellerson said: *"Winning is a habit, and you got to do it all day. You can't just flick a switch on on Saturdays."*

Regardless of your performance arena, taking PRIDE is having an overall system for success.

CLIMBING THE MOUNTAIN OF EXCELLENCE

Climbing The Mountain of Excellence is a symbolic concept used throughout this book. The summit of the mountain represents your goal, a state or national championship, while the mountain represents the obstacle one must conquer to reach it, yourself and your season. The journey up The Mountain of Excellence marks the self-improvement endeavor an individual must take to become a peak performer.

CAIN'S COACHING POINT:
If you want more success on the field, you must become more off the field. Winning a championship is a by-product of becoming a champion.

This book employs the concept of The Mountain of Excellence to demonstrate that the achievement of performance excellence is a long, but worthwhile, journey.

Similar to mountain climbing, football is about training to conquer one mountain at a time. Once that mountain has been climbed, it is time to return to base camp and set your sights on the next mountain's summit and get to work. Each mountain is scaled one step at a time. It does not matter if you are climbing Mt. Everest, one of the big boys, or the local hill in your town - all mountains are summited one step at a time and all football games are won one play at a time. Base camp is your video room, practice field and weight room. The next mountain to climb is your next game.

> "We're living our lives together; we will never again be together as a group this way when this season is over. Never. We all know how things change. We should remember that on every single play. All we need to do is make every play in every game important. Play it as if you'll never play the game again. We do that and then, whatever happens, we can walk away when it's all over and feel good about ourselves and about each other. Every single play. That's what football is. I pledge to give you everything I have on every single play. I want all of you to pledge that to yourselves and to each other."
>
> *Ray Lewis*
> *2 x NFL Super Bowl champion*
> *Future NFL Hall of Fame Player*

ONE STEP TO THE SUMMIT - STAY & YOU DIE

Mountain climbing also serves as a great activity to compare with football because when a team scales a mountain, they cannot simply live on the summit: They must return to base camp, regroup and climb another mountain, or their climbing career is over. Similarly in football, an individual or team cannot win a championship and be champions forever. They will forever be champions of that season, but as soon as the next season rolls around, the slate is swept clean and all the opposition is ready to become title contenders. This forces the champions to start the season anew in their quest for that season's championship, that climb's summit. Therefore, your time at the summit is only temporary.

After The University of Alabama defeated Notre Dame 42-14 for the 2013 NCAA National Championship, somebody asked Alabama coach Nick Saban if he could appreciate what his team had done: three national titles in four years, dominance over a sport we thought could no longer be dominated.

"One day, when I'm sitting on the side of the hill, looking at the stream, I'll probably appreciate it more," Saban said. And then he paused. "But what about next year's team?"
Saban clearly understands that you can't live on the summit. That you must get back on the horse and ride or you will die. After the game he also said that he was going to take 48 hours, enjoy the win

and then get back to work.

CAIN'S COACHING POINT:
It is key that you give yourself a certain time frame to enjoy a win or lick your wounds from a loss. Giving both a deadline where you re-engage back into the moment and into the next game gives you the best chance to prepare and perform consistently at your best.

Ultimately, there is no end to the pursuit of excellence, no one final summit to reach. Excellence is a constant journey that demands personal responsibility in your daily commitment. As you read this book, the use of the mountain climbing analogy will assist your understanding and application of the mental game as you strive to become more.

WHAT IS YOUR SUMMIT?

In reading this book, it is clear that your immediate Mountain of Excellence is conquering this book to understand how to play at your best and achieve performance excellence. How to transform yourself into a peak performer. However, it is only by fully understanding the reasons for embarking on this journey and openly recognizing the larger mountain you desire to conquer that you will make the most of your personal growth and mental conditioning experience. Therefore, you must *begin with the end in mind* to give your journey a greater sense of purpose. You must know precisely where it is you want to end up and *why* you want to end up there, or you might find yourself climbing the wrong mountain - a mountain that your parents or someone else wanted you to climb, not the mountain you wanted to climb.

Think about your desired destination. Is it being the best football player on your team? Is it winning a state or national championship? Breaking a particular record? Getting the college scholarship or drafted into the NFL, or simply making the team? Whatever your journey, you must begin with the end in mind. You must have an outcome goal and a destination to start your journey.

CAIN'S CHALK TALK:
What is The Mountain of Excellence you desire to climb and conquer? What is it you want to accomplish?

_____

_____

_____

_____

_____

_____

CAIN'S COACHING POINT:
Remember, you are allowed to climb more than one mountain, but should focus on one summit at a time. Keeping your mind in the present moment, sticking with the process and staying positive will help you to better enjoy your journey and experience more success than if you mountain hop and pursue different summits during the day. Whatever mountain you are climbing at that time, focus on that specific summit. Be where you need to be when you need to be there, hike one step at a time, and play football one play at a time.

"The journey is better than the inn."

Cervantes

THREE STEPS TO ACCOMPLISHING ANYTHING

Most people have heard the saying "You can do anything if you set your mind to it" but are skeptical of deeming it a universal truth. Well, I am one of those people who believe that if you truly desire something, why not set your mind to it and give everything you've got to achieve it? To make your dreams become a reality you must pursue your goals in an effective and realistic manner. This is why peak performers must understand and effectively utilize the three-step process to accomplishing anything, both in football and in life.

The three steps that give you the best chance to accomplish anything are these:

1. Make a commitment to your goal by writing it down and putting it where you can see it on a daily basis.

2. Make it public and share your goal with your teammates, friends, family, accountability partners and the people in your inner circle.

3. Work with a relentlessly positive energy on a daily basis to make it happen – the type of relentlessly positive energy that can only be found when you are pursuing something you are passionate about and have a reason why. So be very selective about your goals.

These three steps provide you with the strategy that gives you the best opportunity to accomplish anything you desire.

As you proceed on your journey through this manual, utilize these steps to accomplish your process-based goals along the way. This is why you identified and established your mountain in the previous section to facilitate the first step of this process in your personal journey. It is your job to facilitate step number two, and it is the purpose of this book to provide the information and knowledge to facilitate step number three so that you may conquer the mountain and reach its summit.

ONE PLAY/DAY (TODAY) AT A TIME

Now that you have established your mountain and know the three principal steps to reaching the summit, it may still appear to be an intimidating mountain to climb. Do not be daunted by your destination. You chose it because you want it - because a fiery passion within you burns and yearns to shed its light on the snow-capped pinnacle of your mountain. You will conquer your Mountain of Excellence; it all comes down to taking the first step and then another and another until you reach the top. Have patience in the process and enjoy the journey.

INTRODUCTION REVIEW

☐ In football and in life, consistency wins.

☐ If you want to be the best of the best, doing the physical conditioning is not enough. You must do both physical and mental conditioning.

☐ Peak performance occurs only when the body and the mind are working together to maximize their performance potential.

☐ The power of the mind is as miraculous as it is incomprehensible.

☐ Mental conditioning is the process of developing the mental toughness skill set by which an individual exercises and develops influence over his mental state in order to control his physical behavior.

☐ Mental toughness is taught, developed and continuously improved upon, just like going to the weight room for your physical toughness.

☐ Mental conditioning should be integrated into physical conditioning and every aspect of football performance. You do not separate the mental and physical conditioning; you do them together.

☐ PRIDE = Personal Responsibility In Daily Excellence

☐ Excellence is being at your best when it means the most – every single day.

☐ The Mountain of Excellence represents the obstacle one must conquer to reach his outcome goal at the summit.

☐ The journey up The Mountain of Excellence is a self-transformative endeavor an individual must take to become a peak performer.

☐ One cannot live at the summit; you have to keep hiking or you will die.

☐ There is no end to the pursuit of excellence.

☐ Peak performance is a constant journey pursuing excellence and demanding personal responsibility in this daily pursuit.

☐ Choose your Mountain of Excellence you desire to climb and conquer.

☐ Remember, you are allowed to climb more than one mountain, but should focus on one summit at a time.

CHAPTER #1

TAKING PRIDE IN FOOTBALL AND CLIMBING TO THE SUMMIT OF THE MOUNTAIN OF EXCELLENCE

> "Football has been my father in life. Not exactly each coach, but football has replaced my father. It's taught me to be disciplined in whatever I do, be tough, be physical, be mentally tough. It taught me what a man is, because there are so many men within it. You decipher who is a good man and who puts on a front. Football is my father."
>
> *James Posey*
> *Former NFL player*

RISE AND GRIND

Each morning when you wake up, a new climb up The Mountain of Excellence begins. Every day it is time to rise and grind **(#RISE&GRIND).** In your backpack are your experiences and what you have learned on previous journeys from past days. Make your journey by focusing on one day and one step at a time.

The importance of taking one day at a time cannot be overstated. When Urban Meyer was at the University of Florida, he broke the season down to 107 days, not 12 games or 6 months. This was a much more manageable concept for the players and coaches alike. You know your desired destination – the summit of your mountain – but you must familiarize and condition yourself with the fundamental principles necessary for survival. This must be done on a daily basis. Start by breaking the journey down into smaller chunks – winter conditioning, spring ball, summer workouts, two-a-days, regular season, and finally – postseason. *It is the start that stops most people, and the start of your day is the most important part of your day.*

As any mountain climber preparing to ascend Mount Everest can attest, one must gradually build the stamina and conditioning for the long trek to the summit. Putting in the time and establishing mental endurance is of high importance, so that you are prepared for the treacherous conditions you are bound to face on your long journey. **Embrace the adversity** and practice the mindset you need to succeed one day at a time to reach your summit.

WHAT ARE YOUR PROGRAM CORE VALUES?

As you set your sights on the summit of The Mountain of Excellence, you must begin to prepare for your journey by establishing core values. A core value is a personal belief reinforced by how you spend your time and treat other people. You must identify your personal and program core values in order to realize what you stand for both now and in the future. These core values will provide an internal guide to direct you on your journey and will reflect how you approach your pursuit of excellence. These values will provide your safety net for when you fall. And make no mistake - when you hike the mountains that we will, you will fall. **Falls are to be embraced, not avoided.**

CAIN'S CHALK TALK:
Reflect upon the following question: How do you want to be remembered when your last journey is over? What do you want people to say about you at the celebration of your life as a player/coach who was committed to the pursuit of excellence? As you think **about this, write down the core values you will strive to embody over the course of this season and how you want to be remembered.**

_____

_____

_____

_____

_____

CAIN'S COACHING POINT:
Answering the question of how you want to be remembered when your life's journey is complete will help provide clarity to what is most significant to you and how you will want to begin living your life today.

As you reflect upon this big question, consider how your core values transfer to your football performance. Think about how you would like people to acknowledge you and your contributions to your sport and your team over the duration of the current season.

DIFFERENT VALUES FOR DIFFERENT TIMES

The reason we transition focus to a set of core values for the present (off-season into the season or vice versa) and not for an entire lifetime is that a lifetime is a daunting time frame. A lifetime is too difficult to imagine and therefore presents an intimidating mountain to climb. *It is important to focus on how you want to live over the course of the season in order to focus on how you must live in the present moment.* Establishing this perspective will make climbing your mountain appear much more manageable.

Once you have identified what you want people to say about you and you have reflected this in your core values, start living by them "Today." These core values are fundamental principles that should be integrated into the routines of your daily life. If you are not regularly practicing these values, you will end up losing your way to the summit.

CAIN'S COACHING POINT:
The secrets of success are hidden in the routines of our daily lives. You will be as successful as your routines allow you to be on a daily basis. Start establishing routines and habits of excellence.

APPLYING CORE VALUES TO LIFE

When you look to the future, you may think it is difficult to have integrity for your entire life or to be responsible for your entire life or to have self-discipline for your entire life. This may be true, but you CAN live with integrity, responsibility and self-discipline "Today." With this perspective, you have an appropriately sized mountain to climb "Today." And then, do it all over again when tomorrow becomes "Today."

To begin applying core values to your sport and life, choose one or two and focus on them for a set period of time.

CAIN'S COACHING POINT:
I recommend working on your specific core values for 4-5 weeks. Research shows it takes 21-28 days for positive personal change to occur with a focused plan and accountability partner. Right now, look over your core values and ask yourself, "How do I apply my core values in my life at this present time?"

Imagine it is the month of December and one of your core values for December is being self-disciplined. As you commit yourself to working on your self-discipline this month, think about the following:

How would I define self-discipline?

_____

_____

What does self-discipline look like in the different aspects of my life?

If I am an athlete or a coach, what does self-discipline look like in competition, in training, in academics, at the nutritional table, in recovery, and in my personal life?

_____

_____

_____

_____

_____

_____

To provide myself a point of reference and to give me a chance at living that way, how do I identify specifically what it is to be self-disciplined in those areas?

Answering all of these questions is significant to defining exactly what it is and how it is you plan on living this core value. If you specifically outline your core values, you give yourself the best opportunity to live them.

By establishing what it looks like for you to live your core values, you set yourself up for success. **_It is easier to act your way into thinking and feeling than it is to think and feel your way into action._**

Knowing what action you must take and how you will take it to become the new-and-improved version of yourself sets the stage for a successful journey up the mountain.

When establishing your core values, I suggest you focus on between one and three for a given period of time. Initially, setting more than three would be an overwhelming endeavor. Giving yourself a more narrowed focus will increase your chances for successful mastery of a particular core value. If you can focus on self-discipline for the month of December, you are going to have the skill of self-discipline beyond December into January. You may work up to having five or six core values over time. As with most anything, start small, get some summits/wins under your belt, and then go bigger.

SUCCESS LEAVES CLUES

Here is some insight into achieving a successful career in anything you do: *Success leaves clues.* If you want to be a millionaire, go hang out with people who are millionaires. If you hang out with people who are making $50,000 a year and you tell them you want to make a million dollars a year, what are they going to do? They are going to laugh at you, because they do not see it as a reality. If you go hang around people who make a million dollars a year, you will get some ideas on how to make your first million.

The same rationale is true for football. You always hear coaches telling players, "If you want to get better, play with people who are better than you." This is because when you play with better players, you begin to pick up the clues to their success. Imitation and adaptation to higher levels of competition will ultimately lead to performance improvement and success of your own.

> "Associate yourself with men of good quality if you esteem your own reputation, for 'tis better to be alone than in bad company."
>
> *George Washington*

SURROUND YOURSELF WITH BETTER STUDENTS

To further illustrate the importance of hanging out with the right crowd, I will share a personal story from high school. When I was a high school student, I was not great academically. I reached a point where I knew I needed to improve my grades to play college sports. I made a self-improving adjustment in my life and began surrounding myself with those who were academically more successful. I started to study with my football teammates, mainly Tony "Thane" Coudert, one of the greatest teammates of all time, who helped me to become a better student. Rather than go play video games, I would go to his house or the library, and I became a much better student.

CAIN'S COACHING POINT:
If you want more in a certain area of your life, you must become more. You become more by associating with those who are more than you in that area. You will become the average of the five people you associate with most. Pick wisely.

I didn't feel like going to the library, but I went anyway. These students had a pre-established discipline that I knew I needed to develop.

I began noticing their study habits, and I started to learn that there are techniques you can use that are very simple to help with memorization and knowledge acquisition. When I began to imitate them, I started to get better results.

Success is largely about discovering a winning formula and implementing the system that facilitates excellence. Mastering the mental game is no different. If you surround yourself with those devoted to performance excellence, your chances of achieving it will drastically improve. When you invest your time properly into a winning system in the pursuit of excellence, success will take care of itself.

> "If you're bored with life - you don't get up every morning with a burning desire to do things - you don't have enough goals."
> *Lou Holtz*
> *National Championship-Winning*
> *College Football Head Coach*

DAILY GOAL SETTING & TIME PRIORITIZATION

Beyond the establishment of core values, daily goal setting and time prioritization are important for establishing the routine discipline necessary for peak performance. *I used to call it time management, but have since learned that you will manage your time based on how you prioritize your time*; therefore, *time prioritization is one step before time management.*

CAIN'S COACHING POINT:
There is only ONE factor among all the football players in the world who are competing for what you want. You all have only 86,400 seconds in a day. Most will spend time; you will INVEST time. If you are not efficient with your time, the competitors who are will pass you by. Learn to take control and advantage of your time, or your time will take control and advantage of you.

As an aspiring peak performer, you must find different ways to make the best investment of your time to accomplish the daily goals you set. Throughout this book, I will share with you techniques you can use to better invest your time. For example, a great technique for time prioritization is to take a dry erase marker and write on your bathroom mirror what you want to accomplish the next day.

I started doing this when I was in college and have found it to be a VERY effective technique. *When you look in your mirror, you are not seeing who you are. You are seeing who you are working to become.*

You are in your bathroom frequently throughout the day and the writing on your mirror will remind you constantly of what you want to accomplish. It also provides an effective method of preparing for the next day. When you go to bed, you will be relaxed knowing you already have a jump-start on the next day. By simply preparing the night before, your daily goals will always be waiting for you on your mirror when you wake up.

CAIN'S COACHING POINT:
Champions prepare their day the night before. Be sure that you pack your bag; then lay out your clothes, breakfast and everything you need to start the next day with TOTAL DOMINATION before you go to bed.

THREE STEPS TO PERFORMANCE IMPROVEMENT

Whether it is practicing core values or prioritizing your time, peak performance is all about continuous personal development and necessary change. A key theme throughout this book is that if you want more, you must become more.

Championship-winning coaches and athletes know that they must first become champions of personal responsibility in daily excellence before winning championships. They also know this takes an understanding of how to make necessary adjustments to change their performance to attain successful results.

One of the most successful mental conditioning coaches was the late Harvey Dorfman, author of *The Mental Game of Baseball* and mental conditioning coach to some of the greatest athletes in the world. Having spent some time with Harvey, he taught me that there are three essential steps you must follow if you want to make a performance improvement:

1. Develop an **awareness** of what needs to change.

2. Develop a **strategy** for change.

3. **Implement the strategy** with an accountability partner and assess yourself regularly so that the necessary performance change can occur.

Most athletes fall short of significant performance improvement because they either lack the awareness of what they need to change, do not formulate an effective strategy for the change, fail to facilitate the strategy to bring about the necessary change, or have a "YES" partner rather than an accountability partner who tells them the truth. Without this three-step system of performance change, an athlete can never achieve the necessary performance improvement to achieve excellence.

INSTANT AWARENESS

Here's a prime example of the three steps of performance change:

I was working with a player who was 20 pounds overweight. I had the player wear a 20-pound backpack to help develop his awareness of what it felt like to be 20 pounds overweight, and also what it would feel like to lose the extra 20 pounds he was carrying.

He wore the backpack around campus all day and at the end of the day came back to see me. He took off the pack and said he was exhausted. I made him put the pack back on and we went to practice. About halfway through I had him take it off, and after practice I asked how it felt moving around without the pack on compared to how it felt with the pack off. He said it was like night and day.

I placed my hands on his shoulders, looked him in the eyes, and said: "When you shed that 20 pounds you told me you wanted to lose, you are going to feel this good every day. Think about how much better you are going to be." The light bulb went on. He got it. It was a great way to get him to have INSTANT AWARENESS. This athlete went through an experience that immediately conveyed an awareness he would not have had otherwise. This experience demonstrated that, "When I lose the weight, I am going to feel like I do, right now, without that pack on." There is the awareness. Then we came up with a strategy for him to lose the weight. He contacted a sports nutritionist, approached his strength and conditioning coach about his goals, and together they developed a strategy for him to lose that excess weight.

Notice that the athlete did two things: made his goal public and established strategies with multiple accountability partners to assure implementation. Only you can make the necessary improvements; nobody else can make your performance change. It is absolutely essential that you hold yourself accountable to your goals, and the best method is making your goals public. As one of his accountability partners, I talked to him once a week about his goal. After a number of months, he dropped the 20 pounds, became a much better player, was stronger physically and mentally, and realized that with the right strategy and system he could accomplish anything. **SO CAN YOU!**

As exhibited through this example, the change begins with an awareness of what needs to change. Once this is accomplished, a strategy must be developed for the change to occur. Finally, the accomplishment of positive change for performance improvement begins to manifest through the implementation of the developed strategy and consistent assessment with your accountability partners. The three-step process to accomplishing anything, combined with the three steps of performance improvement, provides you with the fundamental mental conditioning tools to effectively and successfully utilize the material within this program.

SELF-ASSESSMENT: STOP – START – CONTINUE

In order to further initiate your personal development and facilitate the accomplishment of your goals, you must assess yourself to build self-awareness. As an aspiring peak performer, you must assess your most recent performances to establish self-awareness of what you must improve in your pursuit of excellence. Take a look at your last three days. What are some actions or behaviors that you are doing that you need to STOP in order to achieve the goals that you have set?

CAIN'S CHALK TALK:
What I must STOP doing in order to achieve my goals:

1)_____

2)_____

Now, I want you to write down what it is you must START doing to help you achieve your goals.

CAIN'S CHALK TALK:
What I must START doing in order to achieve my goals:

1)_____

2)_____

Now, I want you to write down what it is you must CONTINUE doing to help you achieve your goals.

CAIN'S CHALK TALK:
What I must CONTINUE doing in order to achieve my goals:

1)_____

2)_____

The Stop, Start, and Continue activity is a very simple process that ought to be frequently practiced to provide self-assessment and to keep you moving up your mountain. It is a simple activity to keep yourself honest about your work effort, but it is often not performed enough.

SIMPLE vs. EASY

It is here that I will take a moment to address an important distinction in both mental conditioning and performance in general. For any performer, it is important to be aware of a very significant distinction between the words "simple" and "easy." Simple and easy are not synonymous. Just because something is simple in concept does not mean it is going to be easy to do. If all simple things were easy, everyone would perform their best each time out and no upsets would ever occur. There would be no reason to play the game on the field - you could play it on paper.

There are a lot of average people walking around who have excellence buried inside of them but are not trained or not willing to harness their hidden, untapped potential. As you read this book, you must consistently work to adopt and implement the simple practices and techniques that make a significant difference in performance.

THE NEXT 30 FEET

Imagine you were to hike from base camp to the top of The Mountain of Excellence - the tallest mountain in the world. If you were to leave base camp at midnight, could you hike to the top of The Mountain of Excellence on the trail that takes you to the summit? The answer is a definitive "Yes." It will be dark out, but you have the ability to hike the entire way up the mountain in complete darkness because of your headlamp. Your headlamp allows you to travel anywhere in the dark, because it illuminates the next 30 feet of the path. Therefore, by simply focusing on the next 30 feet, it is possible to hike through the darkness to the summit.

When you are hiking the next 30 feet, animals may attack you. You may take a wrong turn, you may challenge Sasquatch with some beef jerky, and/or you may roll an ankle. These events symbolize the adversity you are sure to face on your journey, and they are all outside of your control. All you can do is ***embrace the adversity*** and do what is necessary to reach your destination.

DESTINATION DISEASE

When metaphorically hiking up the mountain, the biggest obstacle we face is our obsession with the end result, the destination. This destination disease is representative of whatever end result you desire – the championship, the starting line-up, a particular stat line, the perfect season or the Hall of Fame. Remember that *the destination is the disease and the journey is the reward.*

Excessive focus and time devoted to looking at the destination beyond the next 30 feet is a common illness. People set their goals too far out in front of them without understanding, creating and implementing a process to get there. By focusing on the outcome, people become stationary dreamers as opposed to advancing toward their goal, 30 feet at a time.

This is, quite simply, inaction versus action: the dichotomy between thinkers and doers. This is the condition of people counting down the days until that dream comes true as opposed to making the days count in a proactive and productive pursuit of that goal or dream. A dream without action will remain a dream, while a dream that motivates action has the opportunity to become a reality.

The game of football is ruled by the relationship between what down it is and the distance an offense needs to cover for a first down. Playing football one play at time requires you to focus only on that distance. On 1st and 10 it's the next 30 feet; on 3rd and 1 it's the next 3 feet. That distance is all that matters!
As you proceed through each chapter of this book, remember to focus on the next 30 feet as opposed to the summit of your mountain. This will prevent you from being overwhelmed at times and will make the ascent appear more manageable. *Keep the process over the outcome and the journey over the destination.*

REFUSE THE URGE TO BE AVERAGE

As you start to apply the strategies in *The Mental Game of Football* to your life, you will receive some criticism, and some people may make fun of you for your commitment to self-improvement and performance excellence. Do not listen to the voices of negativity, for they are the voices of the masses – they are the voices of the average.

Average people and average teams are the best of the worst and the worst of the best. Do not settle for average; strive for excellence and set your sights on the summit. Reach the pinnacle of success by climbing The Mountain of Excellence with a focused determination on your goals and with a dedication to personal responsibility in your daily excellence. *Hike that next 30 feet and you will learn that there are no traffic jams on the extra mile.*

START YOUR JOURNEY WITH ONE STEP

The rest of this book is devoted to the 10-week journey of excellence within the PRIDE program. The material within these chapters will give you the mental conditioning skills to establish your blueprint for excellence. View each chapter as if it is the next 30 feet and conquer the mountain that is this manual. It is a journey that will begin during two-a-days and hopefully culminate with a state championship. Regardless of when you start the journey, however, this program will provide you with the knowledge and skills to make the progress necessary to reach the summit of your mountain.

IF IT IS TO BE, IT IS UP TO ME

Remember, YOUR OWNERSHIP of this program is what will make the difference. You can't just read the book. You must OWN THE BOOK. You must put this book into action.

The most powerful two-letter-word sentence in the English language summarizes what this journey is all about: *If it is to be, it is up to me.* Your success in football and in life is determined by a lot of factors, and no factor is more important than the person reading this right now... YOU!

It has been said that *it is the start that stops most people.* Do not wait. Get started. RIGHT NOW!

Remember, if you take the four middle letters out of "DoN'T WAit!" you get "*DO IT!*"

So don't wait, **DO IT!** Get started on your journey up The Mountain of Excellence, TODAY!

CHAPTER #1 REVIEW

☐ PRIDE = Personal Responsibility In Daily Excellence

☐ Excellence is being at your best when it means the most – every single day.

☐ The Mountain of Excellence represents the obstacle one must conquer to reach his outcome goal at the summit.

☐ The journey up The Mountain of Excellence is a self-transformative endeavor an individual must take to become a peak performer.

☐ One cannot live at the summit - you have to keep hiking or you will die.

☐ There is no end to the pursuit of excellence.

☐ Peak performance is a constant journey pursuing excellence, and demanding personal responsibility is this daily pursuit.

☐ Choose your Mountain of Excellence you desire to climb and conquer.

☐ Remember, you are allowed to climb more than one mountain, but should focus on one summit at a time.

☐ The Three Steps to Accomplishing Anything:
1) Make a commitment to a goal.
2) Make it public with an accountability partner.
3) Work with a relentlessly positive energy today.

☐ Today is where we are, every day.

☐ A core value is a personal belief and virtue reinforced through a commitment to yourself and your team.

☐ Live your core values.

☐ It is easier to act your way into thinking and feeling than it is to think and feel your way into action.

☐ Success leaves clues.

☐ Surround yourself with those who are better than you.

☐ Take advantage of your time or time is going to take advantage of you.

☐ The Three Steps of Performance Change:
   1) Awareness
   2) Strategy
   3) Implementation of the strategy

☐ Frequent self-assessment is essential to establish performance awareness.

☐ Simple and easy are not synonymous.

☐ Focus on the next 30 feet of the task at hand.

☐ A dream without action will remain a dream, while a dream that motivates action has the opportunity to become a reality.

☐ Do not settle for average - it is the best of the worst and worst of the best.

☐ It is the start that stops most people, so get started TODAY!

CHAPTER #2

PRESENT-MOMENT FOCUS
ONE PLAY AT A TIME

> "Taking an enemy on the battlefield is like a hawk taking a bird. Even though it enters into the midst of a thousand of them, it gives no attention to any bird other than the one it has first marked."
>
> *Yamamoto Tsunetomo*
> *18th Century Samurai Warrior*

VALUE THIS PLAY & THIS DAY

The famous samurai warriors of Japan were some of the world's first masters of the mental game. They were taught to "live being true to the single purposefulness of the moment." What the samurai understood very well is that the time is now and the place is here. One of the biggest challenges in life and in becoming a master of your mental game is developing an appreciation for the value in the present and then effectively possessing the ability to channel your performance focus into this present, this day and THIS PLAY in football.

This mission focuses on the present, the first of the Five P's of the PRIDE program. In this chapter you will develop an appreciation for the importance of the present, and you will learn how to develop your present-moment focus so you can compete one play at a time.

In the introduction, you learned about the mindset of peak performers. You started to identify your values and put your focus on the plan as to how you will summit your mountain. You learned the importance of concentrating on the next 30 feet and the process it takes to climb to the summit. As a committed athlete and someone who wants to develop his mental toughness, you must understand that ***you do not count the days - you make the days count.***

How do we actually make the days count? The first step is possession of a present-moment focus.

THE 30-SECOND DRILL

Before discussing the present, I want you to experience it. In the following exercise, I want you to live in the present moment by immersing yourself in a present-moment focus. This exercise was taught to me by my mentor, Dr. Ken Ravizza, and it is called the 30-second drill.

Now as you read this, I want you to invest 30 seconds of your time as if your life depended on what you were reading. Sit up straight in your chair with your feet flat on the floor and LOCK IN! Now, I want you to look at each word and hear it as if I am there inside your head speaking to you.

I want you to read every word with a commitment that if you could regurgitate what it is you just read, you would win a million dollars. Think of it as the Million Dollar Mentality, because when you engage and focus with this type of intent all the time, it will not be long before someone wants to pay you a million dollars to work with them.

Ready?

Give me 30 seconds.

GO!

For a short period of time you can do anything you want with your levels of attention, energy, and focus. Right now, the focus you are reading with is different than it was 10 seconds ago – feel that.

You see, you are more locked in right now than you were 15 seconds ago – recognize that. You are currently demonstrating your ability to be into the present moment and play one play at a time.

If you can focus like this without someone having to ask you, that is the result of a present-moment mental toughness. So, while you read this chapter today, I want you to come back to this level of focus as many times as you can and lock in for 30 seconds at a time.

That is 30 seconds.

You are allowed to space out for a moment.

Whew... I hope you felt the intensity of those 30 seconds.

If I asked you for 10 minutes of total undivided attention with that level of focus, you'd probably say: "Cain, that is crazy. There is no way I can read with that intensity for 10 minutes." I would agree. Break 10 minutes into 20 30-second segments just like a 15-minute quarter in college football is really 30 30-second segments.

Challenge yourself to become a samurai warrior of the mental game, someone who is totally immersed in the present; and when you get distracted or space out, recognize that you are distracted. Then release and refocus back into the present.

FEEL THE PULSE OF THE GAME

When you think of the present-moment focus, compare it to watching a sports performance. For example, if you ever attend a game in a large football stadium and you go to the top row to watch, you will notice that there is a pulse to the game. As the quarterback goes through his cadence, everybody steps into the present. The play is executed. The whistle blows. Everybody steps out.

There is a pulse to the game. There is a routine ebb and flow to the game where the performers, and even the audience, enter the present, play the down, and exit that moment after the play occurs. It is a short, intense focus followed by a space-out. That process repeats itself over and over for about 150 plays a game. Essentially, it is a much shorter version of the 30-second drill the players use as a part of their routine to get into the present moment.

As you read this chapter, you will develop an enhanced understanding as well as the mental skills of present-moment focus. It is important to remember that you can get here, the present moment, anytime you want. It is all a matter of awareness and choice.

"You've got to be able to get back in the moment. It's a sign of maturity. If you go to a seventh grade classroom and something happens and some kid falls down, they'll laugh, the entire class. They can't come back. It's like your lesson plan's done. It's because they're immature little kids. They don't understand you can have a great time but then you can come back to the task at hand. Same thing with mature football teams. Something good, something bad, whatever, we're going to come back and we're going to kill you because we have poise and focus. That's what champions do."

Kris Hogan
Head Football Coach
Faith Christian School
Grapevine, Texas

HOCUS-POCUS or FOCUS-REFOCUS

Realize that success in any endeavor is not the product of hocus-pocus. You are not going to be successful today because the moon and the sun and the stars and the galaxy just happen to line up for you. *You are going to be successful to the degree that you are able to focus and then refocus when you become distracted.*

Success is not hocus-pocus magic; it is actually much simpler than that. Success is largely dictated by your ability to maintain present-moment focus on the tasks at hand. The key to developing an intense and productive focus is to recognize when you become distracted, take a deep breath, and then refocus your attention.

You will get distracted, because everyone does. The attainment of peak performance is contingent on the development of distraction awareness. *You must develop the ability to recognize when you are distracted and then refocus back into the moment.* An easy way to remember this is to think, *If I want to win, I must focus on What's Important Now (#WIN).* Focus on what you are doing right here in this moment and on accomplishing the tasks in the present moment. This is the focus of performance excellence and successful progress.

WATCH OUT FOR FISH HOOKS

Through recognizing that we all get distracted from time to time, it is equally important to recognize what distracts us from our goal. The term "fish hooks" is symbolic of the negative thoughts from external stimuli that your mind can get caught on during your pursuit of excellence.

Fish hooks represent distractions beyond your control that you focus on, which deplete your energy and rip you away from performing your best and living in the present. Examples of fish hooks could be obnoxious fans, poor officiating, unprofessional coaches, irritating teammates, past mistakes, etc. - all of which are outside of your control.

Ultimately, fish hooks are a hassle and a needless waste of your time. You must develop an awareness of them so you do not get hooked, and so that when you do, you can get off the gaff (what they call the barb on the fish hook in the angler's world) before getting ripped out of the water.

To further illustrate the application of fish hooks in performance, think of yourself as a fish. As a fish, you are swimming in a school up Gridiron River to the destination of Lake Excellence.

As you swim upstream, you need sustenance for your journey, so you dine on whatever you can find. You discover worms are an especially delicious but a rare treat. You have observed some of your friends trying to eat worms dangling in the water, only to get stuck in the mouth with a fish hook.

You learn you must be wary of fish hooks when you see a worm. If you accurately identify fish hooks with worms, you can actually still have a meal by eating around the hook. ***Thus, if you keep the presence of mind to inspect your worms carefully, you will give yourself the best chance to reach Lake Excellence, aka play your best in the midst of the chaos called the game of football.***

In this analogy, the worms are the opportunities to learn and succeed on your journey to performance excellence, and the fish hooks are the external stimuli within those opportunities that could keep you from your forward progress. As a performer (or fish), you must stay in the present moment and strategically seize the opportunities for self-improvement. To illustrate the point of focusing on the present moment, longtime NFL defensive coordinator Monte Kiffin told his players over and over: "See a little, see a lot. See a lot, see nothing."

You must focus on what you can control – your presence of mind – and work around the fish hooks that have the potential to hold you back. If you see the worm but forget to check for a fish hook, then you are bound to get hooked.

Be aware of fish hooks. ***Do not get hooked.***

CAIN'S CHALK TALK:
I want you to identify three fish hooks that you deal with on your team. What distractions have a tendency to steal your focus and get you hooked away from the present?

FISH HOOK #1 _____

FISH HOOK #2 _____

FISH HOOK #3 _____

USING CONCENTRATION GRIDS

Concentration grids have been a staple of mental conditioning for years. This game/exercise is all about concentration and efficiency, which is best accomplished by staying in the present moment and going one number or one play at a time. Concentration grids are a great way to increase your ability to stay in the present moment for an extended period of time, as you will need to be able to do to play your best football.

ONE NUMBER. ONE PLAY AT A TIME

Your training program with concentration grids is simple. Cross out the grid numbers from 00-99, in order, as fast as you can. During this exercise, you are testing yourself to see how efficiently you can perform the task. You are also testing your ability to concentrate and stay in the present.

Start practicing this exercise in a quiet environment to become comfortable with the activity and to monitor your present-moment focus. Once you have become proficient at it in a quiet environment, you may play music or do this activity in front of the TV as a way to include distractions, just as there will be when you compete. The more you do this activity and the more quickly you can cross out the numbers in order, the more you are developing your ability to concentrate and keep your mind in the present moment.

Football players I have worked with report that the grids allow them to become more aware of when they start to space out and lose focus in school and on the field. They become more aware of when they slip out of the present and into the past or the future. This exercise also allows them to become more aware of when they are trying too hard and need to take a breath in order to relax and get back into an optimal level of focus.

MEASUREMENT = MOTIVATION

It is also important to keep track of the time it takes to complete each grid. When I started doing concentration grids on a routine basis (Monday, Tuesday, Thursday and Friday mornings before I ate breakfast), my time was in the low- to mid-teens in minutes. After almost two weeks, I was able to do them in about four or five minutes, even in the crazy and chaotic environment known as a high school cafeteria.

Here is a sample concentration grid you can use to help train yourself to stay in the present moment for an extended period of time.

Brian Cain Peak Performance, LLC
Concentration Training Grid
www.BrianCain.com

86	54	04	72	20	05	34	79	52	17
73	43	50	70	44	12	28	59	94	35
45	62	63	97	51	95	91	67	84	75
27	69	23	00	08	83	09	41	65	78
80	39	68	47	29	93	36	30	38	42
61	53	19	48	49	74	40	18	15	21
60	01	14	22	64	07	58	02	32	16
13	31	26	71	66	33	06	85	10	89
76	46	98	37	99	24	57	11	55	82
92	25	81	96	87	88	77	03	56	90

CAIN'S COACHING POINT:

Yesterday is a cancelled check, tomorrow is a promissory note, and today is cash: Invest it wisely.

Yesterday is history. Tomorrow is a mystery. Today is a gift; that is why we call it the present.

CHAPTER #2 REVIEW

☐ Yesterday is history, tomorrow is a mystery, and today is a gift — that is why we call it the present.

☐ Do not count the days; make the days count.

☐ The present moment is a matter of awareness and choice.

☐ Success in athletics is not hocus-pocus. It is all about your ability to focus and refocus.

☐ Focus on WIN (What's Important Now).

☐ Beware of fish hooks and things you cannot control.

☐ Train your present-moment focus by using concentration grids.

☐ The time is now and the place is here.

CHAPTER #3

PROCESS OVER OUTCOME

> "Joe Gibbs and Bill Callahan were right; football was a game of process and the arrival could never be as meaningful as the approach."
>
> ***Nicholas Dawidoff***
> **Author of *Collision Low Crossers***

The ability to perform at a level of excellence on a consistent basis is the goal of all peak performers. As the previous chapter discussed, the maintenance of a present-moment focus will assist you in this goal; however, you must have something to focus on in the present moment during performance. ***This something is the process.***

A peak performer's focus must always be on the process. By keeping focus on the present elements of the performance process, athletes give themselves the best opportunity to perform on the level of excellence. An excellent process will yield excellent results, and performing a step-by-step process directed at excellence will get you up the mountain. Remember, the commitment and concentration on the next 30 feet of the hike will get you safely to your destination. Focus on being excellent on your journey step by step up The Mountain of Excellence and you will be sure to reach the summit.

UNLEARN WHAT YOU HAVE LEARNED

The current football society we live in is a results-driven society. If you are a coach reading this, you will not likely have a job if you do not win games. The kicker is that to win games you must not focus on winning, but on the process of winning. Coaches and athletes I work with most often unlearn what they have learned to focus on in their sport – mainly winning and focusing on other outcomes that are outside of their control vs. processes that are within their control and that give them the best chance for success.

A peak performer must understand that winning is the outcome of performance excellence - thus, the product of an individual's or team's performance. The focus of the individual athlete and team, therefore, ought to be their performance, because that is what is truly within their control and yields the desired outcome. More precisely, a performer's focus should be on the process of his performance and directly on what he can control to provide the best opportunity for success.

CAIN'S COACHING POINT:
You must often unlearn what you have learned and realize that what got you here might not get you there. You must always be asking yourself, *is this the best way*?

THE LAW OF AVERAGES

Former Louisiana State University head baseball coach Skip Bertman was a true Master of The Mental Game and won five national championships in 1991, 1993, 1996, 1997 and 2000. Bertman also hired Nick Saban and Les Miles as LSU's head football coaches when he was the athletic director at the school. Bertman is a man defined by excellence, and he stressed the importance of the process, emphasizing that anytime you compete there are only four possible occurrences:
1. You can play well and win.
2. You can play well and lose.
3. You can play lousy and win.
4. You can play lousy and lose.

Bertman called these the law of averages because if you play your best, you give yourself the best chance to win – BUT you are not guaranteed to win even if you do play your best. *What he knew was that he never had control over the outcome of the game. All he had control over was how prepared his team was come game day and then how they played.* Through this understanding, Coach Bertman knew that the process of performing excellently was what won games, not a focus on winning games. As a coach, he made the law of averages swing in his favor by emphasizing the process of performance excellence and execution on each pitch/each play over the outcome of winning. You can swing the law of averages in your favor as well, if you commit yourself to the process.

THE BEST TEAM NEVER WINS

I have had the wonderful privilege of getting to know and work with Ultimate Fighting Championship Welterweight Champion, Georges St. Pierre. Georges is one of the best athletes on the planet, and a large part of his consistent success has been his ability to stay focused on the process of becoming the best fighter he can be (the journey) while letting go of his desired outcome to be and maintain the status of world champion (the destination).

By focusing on the process of being the best he can be through constantly evolving as he aims for self-improvement and personal progress, Georges gives himself the best chance to retain his World Championship title every fight. Georges realizes that even though he is one of the best fighters, if not the best fighter, on the planet, he can get knocked off the summit of the mixed martial arts mountain known as The Ultimate Fighting Championship on any given night inside the Octagon. He has learned the hard way that *the best fighter never wins - it is always the guy who fights the best*.

"I truly believe that I am the best fighter in the world. And in every sport it is the same story. It is not the best team that wins in football; it is the team that plays the best. It is not the fastest horse who will win the race; it is the horse who races the best. And Saturday night, even though I believe that I am the best fighter in the world, the guy who's going to win the fight is the guy that will fight the best. I am very glad to fight Josh Koscheck. He's the number one contender right now, so I want to get back to what I lost and I will go step by step in the process. I am very happy to fight him."

Georges St. Pierre
Ultimate Fighting Championship
Welterweight Champion
2008, 2009, 2010 Canadian Athlete of the Year
UFC 74 Pre-Fight Press Conference

This quote is from Georges on the eve of his UFC 74 fight with Josh

Koscheck, his first fight after losing his World Championship to Matt Serra at UFC 69 on April 7, 2007. I love what he says about how the best fighter never wins, that it is always the one who fights the best. I hope you can see that he clearly understands the value of the process.

CAIN'S COACHING POINT:
St. Pierre saying "I go step by step" illustrates the mentality and focus on the process as well. When he says, "I am the best fighter in the world," he displays his confidence in his abilities - but he also recognizes that "the guy who's going to win the fight is the guy who will fight the best." This truly emphasizes his mental ability to separate the outcome from what he must do to achieve it. A total focus on the process.

The same logic can be applied to any form of competition. You may be the defending state champion or part of the best program in your area, but during competition between the lines, it does not matter who is more talented or who has a more impressive resume. In the heat of competition, all that matters is who competes at the higher level, who executes and plays better.

If you are the underdog and your whole mentality revolves around you playing your game regardless of the accolades and accomplishments of your opponent, then you have done what I call "released your mental emergency brake," enabling you to play your game at the highest level, one play at a time.

"Let's get something straight right off the bat. We either are or we are not. We're not going to have any triers."

Bear Bryant
Head Football Coach
University of Alabama
6 national championships, 323 wins

WHY UPSETS HAPPEN

To further challenge and change your perspective on the old cliché that "the best team always wins," let's reflect upon some of the great moments in sports history.

The *"Miracle On Ice"* in the 1980 Winter Olympics between the Soviet hockey team and the US hockey team: The Soviet team consisted of seasoned professional athletes while the US team consisted of amateur collegiate athletes.

The whole world expected the Soviet team to come out victorious. The Soviets had destroyed the same USA team in an exhibition game 10-3 in Madison Square Garden on February 9, 1980, just days before the Olympics started. We all know, however, that the end result was anything but what was expected. The US team's 4-3 victory over the Soviets will go down in history, undisputedly, as one of the greatest upsets of all time. Clearly, the Soviets had the better team, but it was the US team that won. Why? **They played better!**

Another prime example that defies the "best team always wins" cliché is Super Bowl XLII between the New England Patriots and the New York Giants. The Patriots had accomplished an undefeated season (16-0) and reached the Super Bowl with a cumulative record of 18-0. This Patriots team was hailed by analysts as arguably the greatest NFL team ever and was the 12-1 favorite to be victorious in the big game. The victory, however, went to the undaunted Giants, who led 17-14 as time expired. Who was the better team? The Patriots. Who played better on that night? The Giants.

Yet another example of a phenomenal upset is the 1985 NCAA Men's Division I Basketball Championship between the Georgetown Hoyas and the Villanova Wildcats. The Georgetown Hoyas were the defending national champions and the No. 1 ranked team in the nation, led by Patrick Ewing, the 1984 tournament's Most Outstanding Player and one of the most dominant players in college basketball history. The Wildcats were unranked in the regular season with a 19-10 record and received an at-large bid as a number 8 seed in the tournament.

In the National Championship game, Villanova went on to play an excellent game against a team most thought to be unbeatable. The Wildcats shot an historic 79 percent from the floor as they defeated the Hoyas 66-64 to become the lowest seed in NCAA basketball history to win the national championship. Who was the better team? Georgetown. Who played a better game that night? Villanova.

In boxing, James "Buster" Douglas, the unknown 42-1 underdog, defeats Mike Tyson. In Olympic wrestling, unknown US wrestler Rulon Gardner defeats Russian wrestler Alexander Karelin, who was previously undefeated in 13 years of international competition. Appalachian State beats The University of Michigan in one of college football's great upsets. The list goes on and on.

All of these upsets are sufficient evidence to conclude that the old cliché "the best team always wins" is false. The main reason is that the more talented teams often get so caught up in the outcome that they forget about the process to achieve what they desire. They shortchange their preparation, and as Super Bowl XLVIII Champion and Seattle Seahawks quarterback Russell Wilson always says, *"The separation is in preparation."*

> "When our players left the room, they were a different team. Why? Because they focused on what we had and not on what we had lost."
>
> *Lou Holtz*
> *Head Football Coach*
> *University of Arkansas*

CONTROL WHAT YOU CAN CONTROL

In 1977, Lou Holtz's Arkansas Razorbacks were ranked #6 in the country and were invited to play in the Orange Bowl against Barry Switzer's #2 ranked Oklahoma Sooners. Unfortunately for Coach Holtz and his "Hogs," two players who had accounted for 78% of the team's points during the season broke training rules. Holtz made the difficult decision to suspend the players from the game and send them home. Even before the suspensions, the Razorbacks were a decided underdog, but afterward the Las Vegas oddsmakers gave them NO CHANCE and the spread ballooned to 24 points! But Holtz was able to get the team to make a critical paradigm shift, getting the players to focus on what the team HAD, rather than what they did not. The result? A resounding 31-6 victory!

A huge part of the process is controlling what you can control (your performance) and letting the outcome take care of itself - and when the "best teams" show a mental lapse, the underdog is usually right there ready to seize the moment. We can, thus, definitively state that the best team/athlete never wins; it is always the team/athlete that plays the best.

The peak performance athletes that best understand the significance of the process over the outcome have established proficiency for recognizing what they can control and what they cannot. It is amazing how many football players still get hung up and hooked on things outside of their control. If you want to become a peak performer, you must learn how to differentiate between what you can control and what you cannot control.
When you put time and energy into things you cannot control, you are wasting both of those valuable resources. Focusing on these things is self-defeating and assists the opposition in the process. Peak performers do not play that way; they stay locked in on what they can control.

Here is a list of things you cannot control in football: You cannot control the officials, the fans, the media, the other team, playing time, the field conditions, the schedule, statistics, coaches, parents and most of all, the outcome of the game. The only thing you can control is yourself and your APE. APE is an acronym for your attitude and appearance (body language); your positive self-talk, presence (focus), process (preparation), performance (how hard you compete), perspective; and your effort, energy and emotions.

FOOTBALL AND THE CONTROLLABLES

One of my favorite sports I use to illustrate just how little control an individual has while participating in competition is football. Football is a crazy game. You can virtually do everything right and still lose. There are also days where you can do very little right and win.

Sometimes, you and your teammates can execute the game plan to perfection and meet the performance goals that the coaches have set for the team during the game, but a bad call or an unfortunate bounce of the ball can completely undermine the team's effort. On the other hand, you can fail to meet your coaches' goals but get a break here or there that keeps you in the game. *Football is an unfair game. So is life. Get used to it, and stop saying "that's not fair."* According to two-time Super Bowl champion head coach Mike Shanahan: "Life isn't fair. It becomes fair only when you realize it is unfair. Once you know it isn't, you're on a more level playing field, and you're better prepared for it." Whining about how unfair things are may get you sympathy from the cheerleaders, but not when you are trying to reach the summit and win on the field.

CAIN'S COACHING POINT:
Are you that bad of a football coach or a player that you have to feel good and have every call go your way to win? If the answer is no, say *SO WHAT, NEXT PLAY* the next time a call does not go your way.

In football, as in life, when you focus on the process of playing the game one play at a time and let the outcome take care of itself, you will give yourself the best chance for on-field and scoreboard success.

Winning is a by-product of executing the fundamentals and focusing on the process over the outcome. You cannot control winning. If we could control winning, somebody would go undefeated every year because they would figure out what it took to do so and then proceed to do it. In the game of football, there are just too many variables that you cannot control. Focus on the process and put yourself in a position for excellence, and the process will eventually reward you with success.

WHAT CAN YOU CONTROL?

CAIN'S CHALK TALK:
As mentioned above, a huge component of the process is controlling what you can control. In the space provided below, write down in the first column all of the things that you can control when playing football, and then list the things that you cannot control in the second column.

CAN CONTROL   **CANNOT CONTROL**

_____   _____

_____   _____

_____   _____

_____   _____

_____   _____

_____   _____

_____   _____

_____   _____

_____   _____

Look at the list of things you cannot control. If you choose to focus on these things, you will inevitably beat yourself. If you choose to focus on these things, you are getting hooked. You must keep your focus on what you can control.

APE

As a peak performer, you must focus your attention on what is within your control. External adversity is a part of life - you make the choice of how you react to it. APE provides you with a reminder of just what it is you have the ability to control.

APE is an acronym to remember that you control:

A - Your attitude and your appearance (body language)

P - Your perspective (how you see things),
the process (how you choose to play), your preparation, your presence (focus) and your self-talk (positive)

E - Your effort, your energy, and your emotions

This acronym is symbolic of the concept "control what you can control." This concept is a fundamental skill of mental conditioning. Self-control is essential to peak performance, and by the end of this program you will fully understand why it is that you only have control over yourself in the midst of performance. As my mentor Dr. Ken Ravizza would say, **you have got to be in control of yourself before you can control your performance** and **you have very little control of what goes on around you but total control of how you choose to respond to it.**

MY GOAL MUST BE IN MY CONTROL

All athletes and coaches will agree that goal setting is a critical part of the process in climbing your mountain of excellence. When setting performance goals, you must remember that **your goal must be within your control. A common mistake made in goal setting is setting performance goals that focus on the desired outcome instead of setting goals that reflect the process that you must execute to get that desired outcome.**

THE TOUCHDOWN PROCESS FOR A QB

In football, a quarterback should not set a performance goal of throwing a touchdown pass (outcome), but should instead set a performance goal of making the proper pre-snap read that gives him the best chance of throwing to the open man (process). Understand the distinction between focusing on the touchdown versus the read. A quarterback's goal should not be to throw touchdowns; execution results in touchdowns. A quarterback's goal is to make the correct read, understand the game time situation, and execute the play in a fundamentally sound manner to result in the desired outcome.

Remember, your performance goal must be within your control. If you are a quarterback, focus on making a play, not getting completions or touchdowns. You could make a great read and a perfect throw but still have it result in an incompletion because your teammate dropped the ball. You should see this as a success because you executed your job - you just did not get your desired result.

You can also make a lousy throw and get a completion, and you should see this as falling short of success because you did not execute your process. Even though you got the desired result, your performance was less than excellent; you did not execute the play correctly but were bailed out by poor defensive execution or a superlative play by a teammate. You just got lucky. By setting your performance goals on making quality plays, you acknowledge and focus on what you can control and give yourself the best opportunity for performance excellence.

By understanding exactly how your game is played – all the real causes and effects of performance within your sport – you can direct your focus to the process of your performance. This knowledge cuts out all the unnecessary elements of the game that most people harp on and gives you a direct route to peak performance. This is what it means to have an understanding of the process when you set performance goals. This is what University of Alabama football coach Nick Saban is talking about when he refers to "The Process."

CREATING AND USING YOUR PERFORMANCE ABC's

One of the most effective strategies to help you focus on what you can control, and to create an effective process to help you play in the present, is an exercise called Performance ABC's.

Performance ABC's are three keys that can be mental, physical, or a combination of the two that you repeat to yourself, visualize, and think about before and during competition. These ABC's of your performance will keep you focused on the process you need to follow to be successful.

There are many things that athletes may think about at times during performance, from physical mechanics to game strategy, to the opponent, to issues in personal life or other distractions happening off the field. Setting ABC's will help keep your mind focused on the proper process for your performance based on the key elements on which you want to focus. This strategy will give you the best chance for success.

Here are some samples of Performance ABC's that I helped create with a top high school football program.

You can see that we set general Performance ABC's
for the program, offense, defense, special teams and coaches. Setting Performance ABC's for the program and units helps give the team a common focus on the process during competition. It also benefits each athlete and coach to set individual ABC's as a way for them to better identify the individual processes they must follow to give themselves the best chance for success.

I challenge you to create your own Performance ABC's for your position group. Choose categories that apply to your position and determine an effective set of ABC's that will reflect the performance demands of those categories.

NAME	A	B	C
PROGRAM	Belief in Self, Teammates, Scheme	Be toughest, most disciplined, most selfless team	30 feet at a time
OFFENSE	Ball security	Win 1st down	Be physical
DEFENSE	Takeaways	Win 1st down	Be physical
SPECIAL TEAMS	Execution of snaps, holds, returns, etc.	Create a game changer	Penalty free
COACH	Be the fountain, not the drain	Focus on your position group during the game	Let 'em play

THE BEST COACHES FOCUS ON THE PROCESS

The best coaches and athletes in football know the value of focusing on the process. They see the process as a staircase they climb each day. They know what their desired outcome is and focus on that outcome 20% of the time, while focusing 80% of the time on TODAY and the steps they must take to get the outcome they desire.

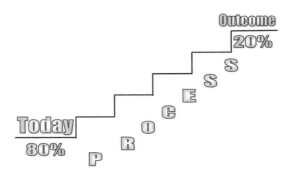

LEE REBELS TEACH CAIN ABOUT PROCESS

In the fall of 2013 I was working with James Morton, a Master of The Mental Game and head football coach at Midland Lee High School in Midland, Texas, in preparation for a game that night vs. the Permian Panthers. It was a scene right out of the movie *Friday Night Lights.* We were walking up a staircase when one of the players called me out.

"Coach Cain, what are you doing?" said their quarterback Caden Coots.

"Walking. What are you doing?" I said.

"I just saw you skip a step, Coach. With all due respect, you can't skip a step in the process and expect to reach the top of the staircase. We here at Midland Lee hit every step on the staircase when walking up to reinforce our commitment to the process."

WOW! I was as blown away as you are. Next time you come to a staircase, hit every step to reinforce your commitment to the process.

SABAN IS A MASTER OF THE MENTAL GAME

One of the most successful coaches in college football is Nick Saban, who won the BCS National Championship at LSU in 2003 and at Alabama in 2009, 2011, and 2012. Take a look at a quote from his book *How Good Do You Want to Be?*

"Becoming a champion is not an easy process... It is done by focusing on what it takes to get there and not on getting there."

"It is done by focusing on what it takes to get there and not on getting there" – **that is committing yourself to the process.**

My challenge for you is to begin committing yourself to the process. Start evaluating your performance on the process it takes to perform at a level of excellence. Focus on the effort you give every day and, most importantly, every play. Focus on executing the fundamentals when you perform in practice and during competition. As a football team, focus on playing with great energy and intensity, supporting teammates from the sideline, and always demonstrating strong body language. All the physical mechanics of your sport and all the elements required for the performance of your sport matter, and performing them all excellently is what makes a peak performance.

CAIN'S CHALK TALK:
What are some aspects of the process that, if you focused on them, would give you the best chance to perform at your best?

1) _____

2) _____

3)_____

THERE ARE NO LITTLE THINGS

It is worth emphasizing explicitly that there are no little things in the pursuit of excellence in football. As alluded to in the previous section, one must also recognize and appreciate all the little details of peak performance within football to become a peak performer. When you are fully committed to the process of becoming a peak performer, you must be aware of all the details of your performance process, for they are necessary to make a successful journey to the summit of The Mountain of Excellence.

KEEP YOUR LOWS HIGH AND YOUR HIGHS LOW

Emotional consistency is essential for on-field success in football. The goal of those striving for success in any arena is to maintain performance excellence day in and day out. The control of emotions is imperative for consistent peak performance.

When you are faced with adversity and your performance is not reflective of your potential, it is crucial to take a step back from your performance and focus on the process of excellence. *Command your emotions by reminding yourself to control what you can control; and focus on releasing the mental bricks that can weigh on your mind by having a physical release that you can use, such as clapping your hands, unstrapping your chin strap, slapping your thigh pad and taking a deep breath.*

Resist the pressure to personalize performance and remember football is what you play, not who you are. By paying attention to the process and not the outcome, you give yourself the best opportunity to achieve excellence, because if you focus on the process and make the necessary changes to it, the result will take care of itself.

The same systematic process is true when you are performing at your best. When you are performing at your highest level and achieving success through performance excellence, it is crucial that you not become complacent. Resist the urge to buy into the hype. Do not think that a little success suddenly renders you more valuable than the process that got you there. Cemeteries are full of irreplaceable men. Stay humble. Continue to work the process. Give yourself the best opportunity to maintain the excellence you have been achieving by identifying the process you followed to get there, and then keep refining that process by making it more efficient and excellent.

On the following page is a "sign of success" from the one of the top college football programs in the country. This image is testament to the program's understanding that you must focus on the process of becoming a champion in order to win championships.

It is challenging to commit oneself to the process of performance excellence. The journey is long and hard, full of obstacles and detours, but this is what makes the glory of achieving performance excellence all the more glorious. *Remember, nothing worth having comes easy. Your enjoyment in the end will be a direct reflection of the effort you had to give in the process of becoming who you needed to become to be worthy of getting what you wanted.*

> "You know, life is basically doing the same thing everybody else does every day. Fulfilling lives come with doing these things with passion, working constantly on the details that no one else but you really sees. It's what we try to pass on to each group of guys we have. It's not just the foundation of our football program, either. Hopefully, in ten or fifteen years, when it matters, these guys will think about something they learned here and make the right decision and have a little success."
>
> *Roger Barta*
> *Head Football Coach*
> *Smith Center HS, Smith Center, Kansas*
> *8 state championships, 323 wins*

DEVOTE YOURSELF TO THE PROCESS

Commitment to the process of excellent performance will give you the best opportunity to achieve your goals. In this chapter, you have learned that when you devote yourself to the process, you focus on the aspects of performance within your control as opposed to the elements beyond it. You now understand that maintaining control of the process of your pursuit of performance excellence is a means to getting your desired outcome and end result.

Unfortunately, it is common for most people in football to become fixated on the goal/outcome/end result of performance. As an aspiring peak performer, focus on what you need to do to achieve the outcome and the results you desire. Devoting yourself to the process of performance excellence will undoubtedly give you the best chance to win and, more importantly, reach the summit of The Mountain of Excellence this season and in your life.

CHAPTER #3 REVIEW

☐ Unlearn what you have learned about winning.

☐ Process should always be placed before the outcome.

☐ Performance Excellence is greater than Winning.

☐ Know the four possible performance outcomes and the Law of Averages.

☐ The best team never wins. It is always the team that plays the best.

☐ Control what you can control.

☐ Develop self-control over your APE.

☐ Winning is a by-product of excellent execution of the fundamentals and focusing on the process over the outcome.

☐ Establish your Performance ABC's.

☐ "Becoming a champion is not an easy process... It is done by focusing on what it takes to get there and not on getting there." – Coach Nick Saban

☐ There are no little things.

☐ Keep your lows high and your highs low – emotional consistency is essential for peak performance.

☐ Make "signs of success."

☐ Nothing worth having comes easy.

☐ When you devote yourself to an excellent process, the result will take care of itself.

CHAPTER #4

POSITIVE MENTALITY

> "I can't stand negativity; it drives me crazy. I've always been positive and always will be positive. When you've lived a dream like I've lived for 73 years, nothing can be negative. My Dad told me one time, 'If you found horse manure in the front yard, you'd go around back looking for the horse.' "
>
> *Tom Moore*
> *Offensive Coordinator*
> *Indianapolis Colts*

The power of positive self-talk and a positive mentality makes a huge difference in an individual's performance. It is a simple concept that is both useful and effective. Having a positive mentality is so simple that it is often overlooked. We're used to hearing people tell us to "think positive" prior to performance or in the heat of competition, but the words often roll in one ear and out the other without our full appreciation of the true value in this all-too-simple piece of advice.

Having positive self-talk (the voice inside your head) with a positive mentality is a mental skill that requires proper mental conditioning to utilize its power. The magnificent quality of positivity is that everyone is capable of it. It is simply a mental attitude that is conducive to growth and excellence through the expectation and perception of favorable and beneficial results. This chapter is devoted to conveying the importance of positivity in performance while presenting you with the strategies you need to develop your own positive mentality.

THE PROPHECY OF THOUGHT

The basic tenet is that whatever the mind expects, it will attract. This "law of attraction" has been proven with neuroscience. Thoughts manifest through actions and affect outcomes. If you are doubtful you will accomplish a task, you drastically increase the likelihood that your actions and effort will reflect that doubt, thus ensuring the failure of accomplishment. Similarly, if you possess a positive mentality when faced with a difficult task, you dramatically increase the likelihood that your actions and effort will reflect that positive attitude, and you will succeed.

The successful accomplishment of a task, however, is not guaranteed by positive thoughts. All a positive mentality does is significantly increase the probability that you will walk away from the task, successfully accomplished or not, with greater experience and with greater peace of mind. In this way, a positive mentality makes a significant difference between educational self-improvement (growth) and self-stagnation (death). Thus, your mentality represents the ultimate self-fulfilling prophecy. Thoughts become things (#TBT).

THE STORY OF ROGER BANNISTER

 On May 6, 1954, Roger Bannister, a British medical student and avid runner, did the previously unimaginable. From the start of archiving world records and modern time- keeping in track events, no one had been able to break the seemingly impassable barrier of the 4-minute mile. His story demonstrates the prophecy of thought and the power of positive belief.

At the age of 25, the British sports media had already discovered Bannister, who had become one of the most scrutinized track athletes in the United Kingdom. His speed in the mile and 1500-meter events drew initial attention to his talent, but when he declined the 1948 Olympics in London to concentrate on his training and medical studies, he drew the criticism of British track enthusiasts. In 1951 Bannister won the British title in the mile, but his fourth-place finish in the 1500-meter race at the 1952 Olympics in Helsinki - the result of a last-minute schedule change that compromised Bannister's preparation routines - fueled further scrutiny for his unconventional training regimen.

After the media publicized his Olympic performance as a failure, Bannister resolved to redeem himself by breaking the seemingly unbreakable 4-minute mile barrier. He increased the intensity of this training, but not the duration, and saw steady improvements in his times, all while he continued to be a full-time medical student. In fact, the duration of his training was less than an hour per day, because he wanted to focus on his study of neurology. Bannister, however, was committed to his new goal and **loyal to the process** he felt would get him there. He was convinced that as long as he continued to see gradual improvements in his times, he would maintain his own training regimen.

The opportunity Bannister had been training for arrived on May 6, 1954, in a meet between the British Amateur Athletic Association and Oxford University at the Iffley Road Track in Oxford, England. Running mates Chris Chataway and Chris Brasher exchanged setting the pace for Bannister's first three laps. Bannister unleashed his kick in the last lap, finishing it in less than a minute before he broke the tape and collapsed in the arms of the gathered crowd at the finish line.

The announcer affirmed what the crowd of roughly 3000 spectators already knew. To thunderous applause it was announced that Bannister ran 3:59.4 - the unbreakable record had been broken and Roger Bannister had made history! He had made the impossible possible.

DEFEATING LIMITING BELIEFS

The 4-minute mile story, however, is not simply about the historic moment of a broken world record. The story of Roger Bannister is about breaking mental barriers and defeating limiting beliefs. At the time, the world of track and field believed the 4-minute mile was an insurmountable human barrier, an impassable obstacle that could not be breached. The critics said it couldn't be done and that it was physically impossible to run a mile under four minutes. It was thought that the heart would stop, the brain would explode, and the lungs would collapse.

As the world scoffed at what it saw as an amateur athlete's unachievable dream, Bannister hardened his resolve to the pursuit of excellence. What makes his feat even more remarkable was that he was dedicated to attain excellence not only on the track, but also in his academic ambitions of becoming a doctor. Bannister believed in himself and he believed in the process to which he had committed himself. As long as steady improvements accrued, he knew the outcome he desired would take care of itself - and that is exactly what happened.

After the myth of the 4-minute mile had been debunked by Bannister, other runners around the world began breaking the 4-minute mile barrier. The week after his historic performance, Bannister and two other runners ran a sub- four-minute mile. Over the course of the following year, thirteen more runners broke the barrier. Within the next two years, exactly 134 runners ran a mile under 4 minutes, and today over 20,000 have been recorded. On July 7, 1999, Hicham El Guerrouj of Berkane, Morocco, ran the current world record in 3:43:13. In 1997 Daniel Roman of Kenya ran two miles for the first time ever in under 8 minutes, in a time of 7:58:61.

This is evidence that there are no physical barriers, only self-limiting barriers. We are the ones who put up these barriers within our own psyche because we choose the beliefs of those around us. You need to unlearn these limitations and realize that once mental barriers are lifted, anything is possible. Peak performers and champions perceive the world differently, and as perspectives change, the realm of possibility expands. My goal for you is to have no mental barriers, to believe you are capable of anything you desire and work toward with the right strategies.

Bannister proved all the naysayers wrong with his positive mentality and self-belief, and now is the time for you to do the same.

> "It is spiritless to think that you cannot attain to that which you have seen and heard in the masters. The masters are men. You are a man. If you think you will be inferior in doing something, you will be on that road very soon."
>
> *-Yamamoto Tsunetomo*
> *18th Century Samurai Warrior*

SELF-IMAGE OF EXCELLENCE

The field of peak performance has substantiated the notion that, as a performer, you will never outperform your self-image. If you believe you are slow, you will perform slowly. If you believe you are fast, you will perform at a fast pace. Therefore, positive thought processes, combined with clear goals and right strategies for how to accomplish them, will give you the best opportunity for success. In this way, staying positive is symbolic of belief in yourself.

A self-image of excellence is absolutely necessary if you are to embark on the quest to conquer The Mountain of Excellence. You must believe in yourself and your ability to improve throughout the process you have established to achieve your goals. You must believe in your inner excellence and its transcendence to the performances you give on a day-to-day basis. Self-image is a powerful tool in peak performance, which is why it is so important for you keep it positive.

INTRODUCTION TO SELF-TALK

When you are playing your best, what are you thinking?

_____

_____

When you are at your best, what types of words are going through your head? What's that self-talk like?

_____

In peak performance, the little voice talking inside of your head, sometimes becoming outwardly expressed thoughts directed at yourself, is referred to as self-talk. During performance, this little voice inside your head talks to you constantly. You may be reading this and thinking: "What is this 'voice' Cain is talking about? I do not talk to myself, only crazy people do that." That would be the voice to which I am referring.

CAIN'S COACHING POINT:
When referring to self-talk, I often use the analogy of your two mental assassins. You

have a green assassin that helps your performance and a red assassin that crushes your performance. You must train your green assassin to win the battle between your ears with positive self-talk.

Everybody has/does self-talk. As an expression of thought, self-talk embodies your mentality towards your performance. We use self-talk to motivate ourselves and to calm ourselves down when stressed. We use self-talk to encourage ourselves to become fascinated and, unfortunately, self-talk can be used to discourage ourselves when we are frustrated. Self-talk is a reflection of self-image.

When you are performing on the field or in the classroom, the voice in your head is either working for you or against you. Some people visualize the contrasting tones of voice as two little people on your shoulders battling for control over your conscience. Recognize, however, that this self-talk is yours. You own it; you are in control of it.

Six-time national champion Bear Bryant understood better than anyone the importance of positive self-talk. He was once asked how some of his most seemingly undermanned teams kept coming away with victories over bigger, faster, and stronger opponents. The Bear's answer was simple and straightforward: "Life's battles don't always go to the stronger or faster man. But sooner or later, the man who wins is the man who thinks he can."

HARNESS YOUR SELF-TALK

Mastering control of your self-talk can be a challenge. Imagine your self-talk is a mustang (not the car, the horse), wild and spirited, seemingly uncontrollable. Now, imagine yourself as a cowboy who does not wish to strip this wild animal of its fiery spirit, but you do want it to work for you to enhance your pursuit of excellence on the open plains - so you must gain control of the animal without taking away its aggressiveness. This is how to think of your self-talk. It is an untamed and powerful beast that has the potential to significantly improve your performance.

Many of the football players I work with describe their self-talk as a high level of aggressiveness but always under control. They often describe it as living and competing on the edge. One player said, "If I am not competing on the edge of my emotions and energy, highly engaged but on the controlled side of the line, I am taking up too much space."

As a football player, your self-talk can be thought of as a:
- Relaxed aggression
- Relaxed intensity
- Controlled rage

To effectively harness your self-talk, you must follow the three steps of performance improvement as earlier discussed. The first step in the process of channeling the power of your self-talk is to establish an awareness of its power over the mind. During performance, try to recognize when you use it and what mentality it reflects – positive or negative. Notice particular situations that bring it out, both the good and the bad. Notice the particular tones and language used. This is all in an attempt to understand your mental state during time on and also away from the field.

Once you have developed a proficient awareness, the next step in effectively harnessing your self-talk is through a technique called confidence conditioning.

FOCUS ON WHAT YOU WANT VS. WANT TO AVOID – THE PINK ELEPHANT

Has anyone ever performed the mind tease on you where they instruct you to focus on something and then say, "Whatever you do for the next 10 seconds, do not think about a pink elephant"? Well, naturally the image of a pink elephant pops into your head and you have difficulty focusing on whatever it was you were told to focus on.

This little mental tease exemplifies the importance of an individual's ability to keep a focus on what you "want vs. want to avoid" because the brain does not recognize the negative connotation of "do not" and only sees the image of that pink elephant.

The key to ignoring the pink elephant is developing the ability to focus on what you are trying to accomplish, not what you are trying to avoid. If you are a football player, think about executing your assignment instead of trying not to get beat. If you are a receiver, think about watching the ball all the way into your hands and saying "catch" as you catch the ball instead of trying to not drop the ball. Academically, when you are taking a test, you want to focus on solving the problem or answering the question at hand, one question at a time, not worrying about the next question till you finish this one. These general scenarios represent the present-moment focus that makes the difference between subpar performance and performance excellence.

By channeling your self-talk and focusing on what you want vs. what you want to avoid, you will be competing with a positive mentality that will keep you locked into the present moment, giving yourself the best chance for success. The ability to focus on what you want with positive self-talk instead of what you want to avoid is a discipline developed over time. This process is dependent on the establishment of routines, such as practicing your self-talk and strengthening your self-talk through the use of confidence conditioning statements.

CONFIDENCE CONDITIONING STATEMENTS

Confidence conditioning statements are a mental conditioning technique used to harness the power of self-talk to work in your best interest. Confidence conditioning is accomplished by simply writing down a list of statements that give you a sense of strength and empowerment when you read them. You can put these confidence conditioning statements on notebook covers, on the wall, on your mirror with a dry erase marker, in your locker, on little cards to carry in your wallet, or set them as the background on your iPhone. You can put them anywhere and everywhere.

Even though you may not be aware of it, you have been using confidence conditioning statements ever since you could talk. Every time you expressed your belief in the truth of an idea or an experience, you were conditioning it. Mental imagery, which is simply the creation of vivid mental images, is a natural process as well. Whenever you imagined something or looked forward to it, you were using imagery and conditioning your subconscious mind. Confidence conditioning and mental imagery are used by a wide variety of people from virtually every walk of life and in every profession. They use these techniques because they are simple to learn, even easier to perform, and they work!

When written and/or put on audio, confidence conditioning statements are your custom-made blueprint for personal growth and mindset achievement, providing a consistent state for your mental imagery and personal development. They are goal statements that help you imagine and realize positive change with minimal stress. If you use them correctly and consistently, they will help you create the athletic career, relationships and life you most desire.

In order to be effective, confidence conditioning statements must be written and used in a way that has the desired impact on your subconscious mind. They must be brief, usually a short sentence, and phrased in the first person present tense. They must be positive, specific and realistic. You want to include as many details as possible when writing and they should carry an emotional charge. If they do not make you feel anything, they probably will not help change anything either. ***The test of whether a confidence conditioning statement is written the right way is to ask yourself, "Can I read, picture and feel this statement?"***

CONFIDENCE CONDITIONING GUIDELINES

The following are guidelines to help you better write your confidence conditioning statements:

First Person: Confidence conditioning statements are tools that help you to change your self-image; therefore, it makes sense to mentally condition for yourself, because your statements are always about you. They will usually begin with "I."

Present Tense: Use the present tense (I am, I have, etc.) because, in your subconscious, the future and past do not exist. Subconscious time is always "right now."

Positive: Condition and image what you want, not what you do not want or are trying to change. Do not phrase a statement in the negative, such as, "I no longer get anxious when I come to the line of scrimmage and know the ball is coming my way." Instead say, "I remain calm, in control and focused on what I want to do on this play, when the game is on the line." This focuses on what you want to do in the present with a positive mentality.

Indicate Achievement, not ability or potential: In other words, do not say "I can." You already have the potential to change your performance. Instead, create words that describe the end result you want as if it has already happened by using "I am."

No Comparisons: You are unique and have your own process of personal development, growth and change. Do not compare yourself to anyone else or measure your abilities against anyone else's. Just aim for and condition performance change in your own self-image and self-belief.

Vivid & Descriptive Language: In order to "convince" your subconscious that your confidence conditioning statements are real, your language and the images they invoke must be as vivid as possible. Be sure to choose words that help you to really "see" what you are describing.

Emotional Language: Use words that spark an emotional response to make your statements more believable to your subconscious. The more emotion you generate, the faster the change you seek will take place. Describe how you feel about your achievement.

Realistic/Accurate: Do not affirm change that isn't possible or realistic for you. Set your sights neither too high nor too low. Stretch your comfort zone a bit, but do not aim for anything you cannot honestly see yourself achieving. Remember, peak performance is a process. Do not aim for perfection; aim for excellence.

Balance: Make sure that the various goals you condition are in balance with each other. Do not overemphasize any one area while ignoring others in which growth would be beneficial. Strive for balanced growth and a balanced life.

Confidential: Without intending harm, others may remind you of your old self-image, or they may feel threatened by your desire to change. Keep your statements confidential. You may confide in coaches/mentors, if they understand the confidence conditioning process and are supportive of the changes you are trying to make for the sake of your performance.

TIPS FOR WRITING EFFECTIVE CONFIDENCE CONDITIONING STATEMENTS

1. Change Your Beliefs Before Your Behavior:

It is pointless to condition new behavior when the underlying beliefs driving your old behavior remain unchanged. Write your confidence conditioning statements for both internal beliefs and external behaviors. Failure to change underlying beliefs is one of the main reasons why confidence conditioning will not work for everyone.

BEHAVIOR: I spend an hour of quality one-on-one time with one of my teammates every weekend to strengthen our bond together.

BELIEF: More pressure on an already jammed-up schedule. I'd rather be hanging out with my friends who are not on the team than with my teammates all the time. When do I get my quality time away from my sport?

Do you see the problem? If the underlying belief does not change, it will be impossible to sustain the new behavior. As long as it feels like something you "have to" do, and not something you "want to" do, your creative subconscious will find ways to get you out of it. Try this as an alternative:

BEHAVIOR: I enjoy spending an hour of quality one-on- one time with one of my teammates every weekend.

BELIEF: I look forward to spending time with my teammates every weekend because it is fun, leaves me feeling great about our team, and is building strong relationships that will help us to perform better on the field.

2. Build Personal Value in Your Confidence Conditioning Statements

The positive emotions you feel as you repeat and picture your statements is what makes them "take" in your subconscious. For example:

BELIEF: My health and fitness are major priorities in my life.

BEHAVIOR: I am creative at finding ways to exercise at least one hour a day, six days a week, and I generally eat only nutritious, low-fat foods.

PERSONAL VALUE: Because I exercise and eat right, I feel energized, strong, in control, and excellent.

3. Review Your Statements To Imprint Confidence Into Your Subconscious

Imprinting is simple: READ or LISTEN to your confidence conditioning statements, PICTURE them in your mind, and FEEL the personal value (positive emotions) connected to them. The best times to do this are just after awakening and just before sleep. Review your statements twice a day at a minimum, although more often is better. Make sure you are relaxed (take several deep breaths) and free yourself from distractions. Limit yourself to 5-10 statements to start – you can add more later. Remember, it is the start that stops most people, so take the initiative and get started NOW!

CAIN'S CHALK TALK:
CONFIDENCE CONDITIONING
WORKSHEET

What do you want to change?

_____

Describe the way it is right now:

_____

Why is it a problem?

_____

How do you feel about the way it is?

_____

Describe your own behavior(s) that you want to change:

_____

What are your deepest beliefs about this situation? Be honest with yourself:

_____

Describe the way it will be after the change(s) you seek (use present tense):

_____

Describe the way you will behave to generate the result you want (use present tense):

_____

What beliefs will you need in order to support these new behaviors (use present tense)?

_____

How will you feel when you bring your vision into reality? What is the personal value for you?

_____

SAMPLE CONFIDENCE CONDITIONING STATEMENTS

If they accurately express your own goals and feelings, use these examples as written or use them as models for creating your own powerful confidence conditioning statements.

Remember, you do not have to confine yourself to just personal and professional confidence conditioning statements; imagine growth in any area of life you choose.

PERFORMANCE CONFIDENCE CONDITIONING STATEMENTS

During performance, confidence conditioning statements become simplified statements for more memorable self- talk. The requirements for these statements are reduced to reflect the importance that they be present tense, positive, and emotional. All other requirements, however, continue to remain relevant. When you are getting ready to take the field, use these confidence conditioning statements to maximize your positive mentality.

SAMPLE PERFORMANCE STATEMENTS

1. I command confidence.

2. I trust in my abilities to execute one play at a time.

3. Today is mine, I own this.

4. I will dominate the line of scrimmage.

5. I have put in the preparation and I am ready to perform.

6. Stay in control, baby - one-play warrior!

7. Let the negative go and the positive grow.

8. Just win this play.

9. Dominate the guy across the line from me.

10. Whatever happens, I will be content knowing I gave my best.

Whenever you read one of your confidence conditioning statements, pause for a moment to picture and feel that statement as it if were happening now. Consciously use the self-talk voice within your head to read and recognize the meaning of the statement.

Confidence is essential to the generation of a positive mentality. During competition, you must be confident in your ability to perform and trust that all your preparation will pay off. This practice of confidence conditioning not only helps you harness your self-talk voice, but it also builds internal confidence so that when the moment of truth arrives on the field, you will believe in yourself and know that when all is said and done, you gave yourself the best chance for success. Thus, the process of building confidence will create the positive mentality necessary for success in your pursuit of excellence.

CAIN'S CHALK TALK:
What confidence conditioning statements, when read on a daily basis, will help you increase your confidence and increase your positive mentality?

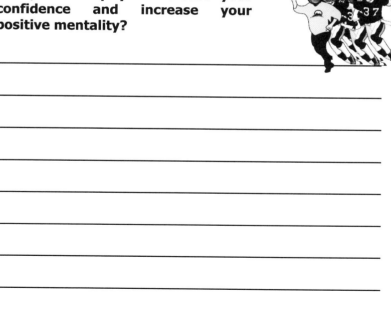

_____

_____

_____

_____

_____

_____

_____

_____

CAIN'S COACHING POINT:
Earlier in this manual we talked about your core values. How are you doing with living out those core values? Are you still setting weekly goals? Your chances for success significantly increase through the simple practice of setting daily goals. Remember, focus on the next 30 feet, working towards improvement and focusing on what you want, not what you are trying to avoid.

THE CONFIDENCE RESUME AND LIST OF WINS

Another strategy for creating a positive mentality and conditioning yourself to be more confident is to make a confidence resume and list of wins. The confidence resume and list of wins is an activity in which you identify all of the wins you have had in your career - wins both on and off the field. The purpose of the confidence resume is to facilitate the development of greater confidence in yourself and your performance by listing all the qualifications that justify why you deserve the outcome you desire.

By nature, we as human beings beat ourselves up when we fall short of our goals and briefly celebrate our wins before we focus on what's next. For example, when you graduated from college, did you really enjoy and take confidence from the body of work you just completed, or were you focused on getting that first job out of school? When you were a child and learned how to ride a bike, did you take confidence from ditching the training wheels, or did you focus on going further and faster? Listing all of yours wins will help you to see the amazing body of work you have done over time and will allow you to have a resource you can review to help build the mental muscle of confidence.

Your confidence resume and list of wins should include anything and everything that, when reviewed, helps you feel empowered and confident. The confidence resume and list of wins should be extensive and ongoing. Like climbing The Mountain of Excellence, the confidence resume and list of wins has no finish line. Your choices can focus on your personal, academic and athletic skills.

They may include previous results, quality preparation, great teammates, books you have read, the people you have met, the places you have been, the wins you have had on the field, the coaches you have played for, doing what was uncomfortable (asking someone out on a date) and celebrating that she said yes, or that you mustered up the courage to ask even though you were turned down (her mistake). Instead of focusing on the no, focus on the process that you asked. ***Remember, you will never get anything in life that you don't ask for.***

CAIN'S CHALK TALK:
Get started with your confidence
resume and list of wins. What are
some of the wins you have had in your
life that you may have overlooked?

_____

_____

Filling out the confidence resume is beneficial for football players because it forces individuals to identify the work they've done and the preparation they've put into the development of their game. This exercise can provide the player with either a confidence boost or a look at a sobering reality. Even if the resume shows you have a lot of work to do, it is important to maintain a positive mentality by realizing you are on the right path and that the resume has given you the constructive criticism you need to get started on your journey. ***Remember, it is the start that stops most people.***

CAIN'S COACHING POINT:
In my work with coaches and athletes, even
the best athletes on the planet can struggle
with developing their confidence resume. That
struggle is exactly why we need to have the
confidence resume in our arsenal as we climb
The Mountain of Excellence. Confidence is
fragile, and every time you review your

confidence resume it will be the equivalent of lifting weights for your confidence and belief. You must do a little a lot to obtain the mental muscles you are looking for. Just as physical muscles take time and effort to develop, so do your mental muscles of confidence.

After you have written out your confidence resume and reasons to believe, post them where you will see them on a daily basis. I have my list on the nightstand next to my bed, and before I turn the lights out, I review my list and go to sleep feeling like a champion. Having this document visible will give you confidence by seeing you have reasons to believe in yourself. Some teams I work with will create a confidence resume for the season and review it before each game to remind the team of the hard work and preparation they have invested so that they should have confidence.

This daily and/or pre-game action is like strength and conditioning for your mental game. Through the repetitious acknowledgement of your reasons to be confident, you will steadily build a stronger, more confident mentality. During competition, this should be reason enough to stay positive while you embrace the adversity that football brings every day.

SOURCES OF CONFIDENCE

Confidence conditioning will improve positive self-talk, and the confidence resume will augment your belief in yourself and a positive mentality. Both techniques of confidence building rely on a solid base of preparation. True and authentic confidence comes from the combination of actions an individual takes in preparation for performance. Confidence comes from these four key areas:

1. Physical preparation – the BST (Blood, Sweat, and Tears)

2. Positive self-talk & confidence conditioning

3. Performance routines you have to keep you consistent

4. Mental imagery of you performing at your best

There is no substitute for smart, hard work. The consistent implementation of effective mental conditioning with your physical conditioning will give you the biggest confidence boost. Physically, you would never do strength and conditioning once a week or once a semester and expect to get any stronger. The same rules apply to mental conditioning and by integrating it into your physical conditioning, you get the most out of mind and body. Strengthening and conditioning to enhance your mental confidence is obtained by doing a little a lot, not a lot a little. Every time you grind it out in practice and give that extra effort, and every time you take the opportunity to reflect on your confidence conditioning statements and your confidence resume, you build the mental muscle of confidence.

Conditioning self-confidence is all about building a positive mentality. When it comes down to your performance, all you can do is rely on your preparation and execute in a manner that gives you the best opportunity for success on that play. You cannot control anything else. You must strive for excellence in practices and games one play, one rep at a time to give yourself the peace of mind that you have done your best to give your best; the rest will fall into place.

KEEP YOUR CONFIDENCE HONEST

A great way to keep your confidence honest is through the utilization of an accountability partner(s). There are many different ways for teammates to keep each other accountable for building confidence. Feel free to arrange whatever methods you feel will serve you best in your program. One great way to keep your confidence honest is for your accountability partner to ask you questions about your confidence whenever you see each other. As teammates, if you see each other walking to class or in the dining hall, ask "Can you tell me two things on your confidence resume?" "What are three of your confidence conditioning statements?" If you do not respond within a few seconds, then you know you are not reviewing and giving enough focus to your mental conditioning techniques.

During practices, the question I ask players all the time is, "What are you working on today to get better?" If they cannot answer me quickly, they have not properly prepared for practice. They are not present and are not getting the most out of their time at practice that day. They are not building mental confidence and are not building a positive mentality necessary for performance excellence.

> "We have learned more over the years from losing than from winning. And the knowledge we have gained from those losses has helped us win more games."
>
> *Jim Tressel*
> *Former Head Football Coach*
> *Ohio State University*

FAILURE IS POSITIVE FEEDBACK

In your pursuit of excellence, you will experience failure. This is a fact. Nothing worth having comes easy, and no self-made success story is created without trials and tribulations to overcome. Accept failure as an inevitable part of your journey and learn to view failure as positive feedback.

Failure is actually the most effective form of positive feedback. Failure provides you with the most direct and honest insight into why and how something has gone wrong. If you are trying to accomplish a task and are giving it your best effort, exercising various techniques but are failing, then you are receiving positive feedback from the task on what not to do. This is when you should become fascinated, not frustrated, and realize with each attempt you are exposing the details that will lead you to success.

Remember the prophecy of thoughts, and how your positive or negative thoughts manifest through actions and outcomes. Be positive. Be confident. *Confidence is a choice.* Challenge your limitations and move beyond your mistakes and shortcomings by learning from them. *In life there are winners and learners.* The quicker you make mistakes and learn from them, the quicker you move beyond them and the more prepared you are for the next 30 feet. Choose to be a learner, not a loser, and get better, not bitter. Accept failure as positive feedback.

CAIN'S COACHING POINT:
It is important to have the capacity to distinguish when you are getting closer to success and when you are moving further from it. Be sure to ask for advice or counsel when necessary, but be aware

that this is your journey. Also, remember that sometimes when the accomplishment you desire feels far away, it actually may be waiting right around the corner.

THE THREE MAGIC LETTERS – YET

When you experience a disappointment in performance and the result you worked so hard to achieve falls beyond your reach, there is a three-letter word to keep your positive mentality – "YET." You can turn statements of failure into goal-setting exclamations by adding this simple three-letter word. This word will turn negative comments around and change your attitude, confidence and perspective. When you notice you are telling yourself (self-talk) that you cannot do this or that, add the three magic letters "Y-E-T" to the end of your sentence.

I am not in the starting lineup... YET.
I cannot read the option... YET.
I do not squat 450... YET.
We didn't win the championship... YET.

By adding "YET" to the end of your sentence, you leave the door to your mental hall of excellence open as opposed to slamming the door in your own face. YET is also an acronym for Your Energy Talks, referring to the influence of your energy on yourself, your team and your goals. When the mood is down and thoughts are negative, use this acronym to remind yourself or others to change the outlook of the situation. Disappointments will occur in your performances, but treat failures as positive feedback and learning opportunities to work smarter and harder, and keep a positive mentality.

POSITIVE ENERGY IS CONTAGIOUS

Energy is contagious. Is yours worth catching?

People subconsciously take cues from others to gauge their own feelings. You probably know when your friends and teammates aren't feeling 100 percent even before they tell you, maybe even before they are aware of it. You definitely know when people are feeling great, because they often exude an aura of positivity that is difficult to ignore. Whether through an outward expression of body language or just feeling a vibe, humans are exceptional at interpreting moods. For better or worse, we are so proficient at detecting moods that we often subconsciously take direction from them and mimic that energy in our own actions. The importance of energy in performance should be quite clear.

If energy is contagious, it is obvious you should make that energy positive. *If you are a head coach reading this, your energy is THE MOST CONTAGIOUS.* Tom Osborne, who won two national championships at the University of Nebraska, commented in his book *Faith in the Game* on how important it is for coaches to stay positive around their team: "More often than not, players will play up or down to the level of confidence the coach displays in them. I believed it was very important that the comments our coaches made about our football team reflected a confident attitude toward our chances of winning. If players sense their coaches don't have faith in them, they will often turn their coaches' concerns into a reality."

Negative energy is simply counterproductive and detracts from gaining momentum for forward progress. A positive attitude when facing the challenges and obstacles of practice or competition goes a long way. Attitude reflects leadership, and if you perform with a positive attitude and bring positive energy on a daily basis, the atmosphere of your team and working environment will begin to reflect your commitment to positive energy. Therefore, if energy is contagious for producing attitudes and attitudes reflect leadership, then leadership, too, is contagious. As you perform, make a concerted effort to build a team of leaders by bringing positive energy to the table.

GET BIG

The term GET BIG refers directly to body language in relation to peak performance. It means to convey a big, confident body language. As you walk down the hall, on the floor of the weight room, on the field or into your office, your body language is an expression of yourself and conveys a message to those around you.

What happens physiologically and psychologically as you GET BIG is that your brain and body will start to release chemicals that will make you feel more confident. You will start to come up with reasons why you should feel more confident, and you will become more confident. Psychology and physiology form a two-way street. You will affect your physical performance by how you think and talk to yourself, and you will affect your psychology by how you carry yourself physically, all the while reinforcing a positive self-image.

I have found that it is easier to act yourself into a way of thinking than it is to think yourself into a form of acting. You must practice GETTING BIG by consciously walking BIG, and reinforcing confidence by self-talking BIG. GETTING BIG will help you to find the confidence you need to perform at your best. One team I worked with that won an NCAA National Championship understands the importance of GETTING BIG and uses signs of success in their facility and locker room to remind them of this key peak performance principle.

CAIN'S COACHING POINT:
Where will you hang a GET BIG sign where you can see it each day?

SELF-TALK – FINAL THOUGHTS

During performance, your "final thought" symbolizes the last conscious thought in your head before performing a specific action on that play. The moment before the ball is snapped, you want to narrow your mental focus on a word or phrase that mentally facilitates the physical accomplishment of that action. This final thought should reflect a positive mentality and affirm confidence to intensify your focus on the task at hand and thus increase the likelihood of its successful execution.

Too often athletes focus on what they want to avoid, rather than what they want to accomplish. Legendary college football coach Lou Holtz tells the story of how he unwittingly poisoned his quarterback's chances of success during a critical game while he was at Notre Dame. Late in the first half with the game tied, Notre Dame was threatening to score and Holtz called a timeout. Here was the scenario before his quarterback went back on to the field: "I looked him in the eye and said, 'We've got three points on the board, so don't take them off.' This was like telling a place kicker to not miss wide right." **When the last thought you give an athlete is negative, negative things usually happen**.

"Rather than telling the QB, make a good decision and let your talent handle the rest," Holtz said, "I left him pondering the negative. As a result, he threw an interception, and we went into halftime with the score tied."

Develop your own final thoughts for particular performance actions. Once you have chosen them, you want to incorporate these final thoughts into your performance routines to enhance the mind-body performance connection. Mentally conditioning a final thought will establish confidence by building a routine rhythm to your performance and pre-snap routine. Developing your own final thought process will undoubtedly help give you the best opportunity for performance excellence on each play.

CAIN'S CHALK TALK:
What are some final thoughts that
you could use in your performance?

1)_____

2)_____

3)_____

REALISTIC POSITIVITY

A positive mentality alone will not grant you performance excellence. Do not get carried away with the thought that a positive mentality is the sole element of success, because positivity alone will get you nowhere - you must still take massive action. A positive mentality is, however, essential to the development of a present-moment focus on the process and play and your overall perception of performance and life. Positive people do better in the face of adversity, and football is a game of adversity.

CHAPTER #4 REVIEW

☐ Thoughts manifest through actions and affect outcomes.

☐ A positive mentality makes a significant difference between educational self-improvement and self-stagnation.

☐ Defeat limiting beliefs with a positive mentality.

☐ Keep a positive self-image.

☐ Self-talk is a reflection of self-image.

☐ Harness your self-talk through confidence conditioning.

☐ Your confidence conditioning statements build a positive mentality.

☐ Confidence resume facilitates development of confident performance.

☐ Keep your confidence honest by utilizing an accountability partner.

☐ Failure is positive feedback; get better, not bitter.

☐ Turn statements of failure into goal-setting exclamations by adding YET.

☐ YET - Your Energy Talks.

☐ Energy is contagious, so make yours positive.

☐ GET BIG with your body language and self-talk.

CHAPTER #5

CHAMPIONSHIP PREPARATION

> "The will to prepare to win is even more important than the will to win."
>
> *Vince Lombardi*
> *2-time Super Bowl Champion*
> *Hall of Fame Coach*
> *Green Bay Packers*

In 2004, the California State University, Fullerton baseball team completed the first half of their season with a 15-16 record. At this midway point in the season, the team made the collective promise to turn their season around by placing their collective faith and trust in their preparation. In one of the greatest single-season turnarounds in college baseball history, Cal State Fullerton would go on to win the NCAA Division I National Championship with a final record of 47-22.

The Titans and their head coach George Horton were able to turn their season around with a commitment to the fundamentals and an intense focus on preparation, both physical and mental. I was a member of the Fullerton staff in 2002 and 2003, and I know firsthand that Coach Horton is a firm proponent of competing every day in practice as if it were a national championship game. I've seen firsthand how to replicate championship intensity in practice with proper structure and commitment to the preparation process.

When the team reached the College World Series in Omaha, Coach Horton brought a water bottle filled with dirt from the team's field in Fullerton. Before the start of the College World Series, the team went out onto the field and sprinkled that Fullerton dirt on the mound and in the batter's box of Rosenblatt Stadium, Official Home of the NCAA College World Series. This action served as a reminder to his players of all the hard work and preparation put in every day of practice back home, and that performance on the biggest stage of college baseball was no different than back home.

The game remains the same anywhere you play - nothing changes.

It reminded players that the goal was to do the same thing in Omaha that they did every day in Fullerton – to continue to play against themselves and the game, throw quality pitches, have quality at-bats and play quality defense. It reminded the team that they compete as hard as anyone in the country on a daily basis in practice and that is what they were going to do in Omaha – nothing changes. It was clear that Horton and the Titans trusted their preparation, because the result took care of itself.

Although this is a baseball example, it could have just as easily been a football example. Playing one pitch at a time is no different than playing one play at a time in football. Focusing on preparation and what you can control will give you the best chance for success on the diamond, on the gridiron and in life.

CHAMPIONSHIP PREPARATION

Legendary Alabama football coach Paul Bryant wrote in *Building a Championship Football Team* that his practices were so hard, so fast-paced and so competitive that when Alabama played against other universities his players would often remark that it felt like the games were in slow motion. It seemed this way because the tempo of these games was, in fact, slower than their practices. When the teams stepped out onto the field, Coach Bryant's practice philosophy gave his team a psychological edge over the competition. And as the Bear's six NCAA national championships confirm, his practice philosophy was the epitome of championship preparation. Gene Stallings, one of Bryant's players in his days at Texas A&M who went on to win a national championship of his own as a coach at Alabama, had this to say about playing for the Bear: "To him, the game *was* practice. If you practiced harder and better than the other teams, you won. All of us, including the guys who were talking about quitting early in the season, learned that the games were easy compared to the practices. In comparison, the games were fun."

MENTAL PREPARATION

Mental preparation is fundamental to peak performance. In the words of John Wooden, "Nothing is better preparation for intense game pressure than countless hours of disciplined effort spent mastering the fundamentals." In this chapter, we focus on mastering the fundamentals of mental preparation through the implementation of effective mental conditioning practices and techniques.

Performance reflects preparation, and these strategies aim to cultivate a peak performance mentality as you practice for your performances, as well as the practices of your daily life. This chapter will help you establish a disciplined effort in developing a lifestyle of performance preparation.

GAME-LIKE PRACTICE

Game-like practice is essential for enhanced mental preparation. If you want to perform at a level of excellence, you must practice at a level of excellence. Practice is performance. The dictionary definition of "practice" is "to perform (an activity) or exercise (a skill) repeatedly or regularly in order to improve or maintain one's proficiency." This definition illustrates what peak performers must internalize: ***Repetition of quality performance is fundamental to the achievement of excellence in football, in life.***

Coaches are always telling players that "You will play like you practice, so you should practice like you play." This is contingent, however, on making practices game-like. The purpose of game-like simulations is to help familiarize players with the conditions they will face in the heat of competition. Repeated exposure to game-like conditions is the best method to mentally condition for the real game. When your time comes to perform on the big stage, if you already put in the hard work to accustom yourself to the environment, it will pay off through your performance.

PRACTICE HALFTIME

In preparation for Super Bowl XLVIII, Seattle Seahawks head coach Pete Carroll actually had his team practice halftime. Halftime of a Super Bowl is almost twice as long as halftime of any other game during the season. Carroll felt it was important to practice the extended time of sitting around so that on game night it would not be the first time his team had to experience the extended layoff and then gear it back up for the second half. Great football coaches will also practice time-outs, the national anthem and where they will meet in the locker room for pre-game and halftime preparations.

The celebrated 20th-century American author Ray Bradbury said: "I know you have heard it a thousand times before. But it is true – hard work pays off. If you want to be good, you have to practice, practice, practice. If you do not love something, then do not do it." This sentiment is dead on. If you have the love and desire to be excellent at football, practice is a positive, not a negative. NFL secondary coach Dennis Thurman, who won a Super Bowl with the Baltimore Ravens, believes this: "True champions hold people accountable to a championship standard. It's hard to do. Winning the title will be the hardest thing you'll ever do in your life because everybody wants the same prize." To reach this high level, practice must be of proper quality to render desired results. Repetition of a poor-quality performance will result in just that, whereas excellent quality will produce performance excellence. Remember, repetition alone does not bring rewards; it is the quality and game-likeness of preparation that brings quality performance.

REWARDED BEHAVIOR = REPEATED BEHAVIOR

Extensive research in developmental psychology espouses that rewarded behavior becomes repeated behavior, true for both poor and quality behavior. By rewarding specific steps in the preparation process when executed properly, the development of skill proficiency is enhanced. Coupled with simulated competition in game-like practices, players place themselves in the best environment to cultivate performance excellence.

What a player wants to hear most is his name attached to a specific positive compliment. As you pass out praise to your teammates, the more specific you can be, the more beneficial the impact of that praise. Telling Brian that he did a good job means very little because Brian does not hear exactly what he did to receive the positive compliment. Telling Brian that he did a great job in pursuit after he was knocked down by a cut block and was then in position to recover a fumble well downfield rewards him for his hustle and relentless pursuit. This will yield more of the same effort in the future. Through this positive reinforcement, rewarding proficiency will ultimately improve performance.

STRATEGIES FOR GAME-LIKE PRACTICE

1. **Make it competitive** – have a winner and loser for everything. If there is a winner and loser when you play in competition, structure that same competitiveness within your daily practices so that everything you do simulates that competitive intensity. Athletes love competition, so giving athletes more opportunities to compete will increase intensity and enhance development. Giving each player an individual win/loss record for competitions held each day and then posting these win/loss records so that they can be seen each day help to show who the best competitors and best winners are in your program. Competing against each other sets standards of excellence in practice that will help take your practice competitiveness to the next level.

2. **Different-colored practice uniforms** will help to create a separation between the two teams and give the practice a more competitive flavor. When you put the practice uniform on, it becomes part of your routine and helps an athlete's segmentation from school (boy scout mentality) into football player (bounty hunter mentality). Athletes also appear more uniform when in uniform, which seems only appropriate. This emphasizes the importance of the team as a unit, setting the stage for the collective "we" over the individual "me."

If you can break out your game uniforms, this is a great opportunity for each player to see if his uniform fits comfortably and does not hinder any physical movements. It also helps create that competitive environment of two teams going head-to-head to enhance competition.

3. **Bring in officials when you scrimmage**: This will free up coaches and athletes on your team from having to make the calls. It will also increase the competitive nature of the scrimmage because it is more game-like.

4. **Use a scoreboard** so that the coaches and athletes can keep track of the stats just as you would in competition. Creating a process-based scoring system in which you give points for specific aspects of performance is also a great way to reward the behavior

you want in your team. For example, giving three points to the team whose player makes a great downfield block in a scrimmage will reward the type of behavior desired in games. It will also give instant feedback to the team that a great block is worth as much as scoring play.

PROCESS-BASED SCORING SYSTEM

A strategy to make practice more game-like is to create a process-based scoring system for intra-squad scrimmages. Under the premise that rewarded behavior becomes repeated behavior, points are earned for a player's effort and execution of particular skills rather than just points for scoring a touchdown or kicking a PAT.

Coaches often choose to use process-based scoring systems during practice to highlight particular skills in which the team must improve. I often recommend coaches begin using this system to focus on one particular skill at a time. As players familiarize themselves with the framework of the system that the coach has implemented, the coach may introduce and highlight more skills to monitor. This process-based scoring system is, like all systems of preparation, one of steady progression. Coaches may even add different dimensions to the scoring system, such as taking away points or giving points to the other team for anything seen as disrespect in the game.

Below is an example of a process-based scoring system for football:

DEFENSIVE

TOUCHDOWN – 12pts

TURNOVER – 4pts

3 & OUT – 3pts

DRIVE STOP – 2pts

SACK – 2pts

TACKLE FOR LOSS – 2pts

FORCE FUMBLE – 1pt

OFFENSIVE

TOUCHDOWN – 6pts

FIELD GOAL – 3pts

15-YD RUN PLAY – 3pts

20-YD PASS PLAY – 3pts

2-PT CONVERSION – 2pts

FIRST DOWN – 1pt

EXTRA POINT – 1pt

SPECIAL TEAMS

BLOCKED FG – 3pts

BLOCKED XPT – 1pt

PIN INSIDE 20 – 1pt, INSIDE 10 – 2pts, INSIDE 5 – 3pts

CAIN'S COACHING POINT:
The process-based scoring system can be changed to fit your program needs, and you can award points for any part of the process that you wish to emphasize.

I've seen these process-based scoring systems implemented to encourage performance excellence in everything a team does during preparation. If there is a non-hustle play, two points go on the board for the other team. If there is team energy with involvement, such as players getting excited for a great block, they get two points on the scoreboard for energy and engagement, because energy and engagement are two very important parts of the process of playing championship football. After the change of possession, if the units get off and on the field in ten seconds, points are awarded because getting on and off the field is significant in doing little things excellently. It is the little things like getting on and off the field that look good but, more importantly, they add pace and tempo to the game and give you a competitive advantage.

> "I'll show highlights of players on our team who I thought had made a really great effort in the previous game. These aren't the flashy highlights. Instead, I show about six routine plays that led to good results because of the great effort we gave. The point here is that giving your best effort will pay big dividends to the team."
>
> *Mike Leach*
> *Head Football Coach*
> *Washington State University*

EXTRA EFFORTS OF EXCELLENCE

To further emphasize the significance of excellent preparation in all things, no matter how small, let's explore the importance of extra efforts. By elaborating on the importance of the aforementioned example of getting on and off the field in a timely manner, the crossover effect from preparation to competitive performance becomes clear. For example, if you are facing a powerful offense, you want to make sure that your defense is on the field as soon as possible so that they have the most amount of time pre-snap as possible. The extra effort to get on the field quickly gives your team more time to adjust to the personnel groupings, shifts and motions that you may have to deal with during the possession, and should become a routine element of your in-practice performance that transfers to game time.

This example of extra effort applies to the other side of the ball as well. It is critical for an offensive unit to control the rhythm and tempo of the game. If they hustle onto the field, get the play call from the sideline as soon as possible and get up to the ball ready to go, it is possible to catch the defense unprepared, scrambling around trying to keep up with your pace. This instantly puts the defensive team on their heels and gives you the advantage. Extra effort can make them uncomfortable and therefore more likely to make errors in execution.

PRACTICE MAKES PERMANENT

Practice does not make perfect; practice makes permanent. It is the quality of your practice that gives you the best chance for quality performance. If your practice is high or low quality, you can be certain your performance will reflect it. Also, notice that I am highlighting quality instead of quantity. I mentioned the value of quality repetition earlier, and it cannot be overemphasized. You can practice something all day long, but if you have practiced the wrong technique, all that preparation means little. It is not the quantity, but the quality that counts. This is also why proper mental conditioning is so significant, because if you do not exercise a winning mentality, you are bound to lose.

It is your obligation in your pursuit of excellence to utilize your preparation time to make the right skills permanent. As athletes, we do not often, if ever, have control over the situations in competition. In practice, however, the control is ours. In practice, you control the repetition of rehearsing plays and running through game-like scenarios. In practice, you can try something over and over again. Take advantage of that time, because we all know that when game time rolls around and the stakes are elevated, you only have one shot to get it right. This is also why elevating the level of practice to simulate game-like intensity is beneficial. Recognize that practice makes permanent; control the quality of preparation – it will determine how you perform.

PAY ATTENTION TO DETAIL

The practice of mental preparation is founded on attention to detail. When you give the little details the same treatment as the larger ones, you give yourself the most opportunities to employ techniques of the mental game. ***Excellence in small things is excellence in all things.***

This applies not only to when you practice your sport, but to cultivating your mental preparation through daily actions representative of that preparation mentality. With the adoption of this lifestyle, the practice of mental conditioning becomes routine and this perspective becomes habit. Daily tasks become performance preparation. All the more reason to seize the day, and take PRIDE (Personal Responsibility In Daily Excellence) in your preparation.

BIT BY AN ELEPHANT?

Have you ever been bitten by an elephant? What about a mosquito? My guess is that you have never been bitten by an elephant but have been bitten by plenty of mosquitos. Please understand football and life are the same way. It is the little things that add up over time. It is not the BIG elephants that keep us from achieving excellence; it is the small daily decisions, the metaphorical mosquito bites that either take us where we want to go or hold us back.

PERFORMANCE INTENSITY

If you want to improve your performance in games, the best way to begin is to start increasing the intensity of your practices. This can be accomplished by increasing the tempo and pace in practice. As we learned from Coach Bryant at the beginning of the chapter, the harder and faster you compete in practice, the more comfortable you feel in games. Award-winning author Jon Gordon wrote in his book *Training Camp:* "What greatness really requires is a willingness to be uncomfortable. Here's the deal. If you are always striving to get better, then you are always growing. And if you are growing, then you are not comfortable. To be the best, you have to be willing to be uncomfortable and embrace it as part of your growth process." *You must learn in practice to get comfortable with being uncomfortable.*

If you can make decisions and actions happen faster in practice than in games, you are giving yourself the best chance to play at your best against teams or players who have more talent. When you face these opponents, the pace of the game tends to speed up. If you practice under up-tempo conditions, you will be more capable of holding your own, because you will have established — mentally and physically — the endurance and stamina through your preparation.

Remember, tempo and pace are measured under time. Find ways you can use a stopwatch in practice to pick up the pace of play and make your pace of play faster than it will be on game night.

BE QUICK, BUT DO NOT HURRY

One of Coach Wooden's great maxims was the advice, "Be quick, but do not hurry." This is significant because you want to increase the tempo of practice without compromising the quality of the practice. This is an important balancing act in your performance preparation. If you work too fast, the more mistakes you will make and the less you improve your game. This rule is applicable to the development of both physical skills and mental skills.

Coach Wooden's advice, however, serves as a warning to those who want to shortcut the process. Before you increase the intensity of performance, you should be proficient in the fundamental skills necessary for such performance. This seems intuitive, but when people hurry to play at the highest level, they often run headfirst into the brick wall of reality — the reality that there is no shortcut to excellence. This is why it is important to make sure to practice technique before you increase tempo. It is good to be a quick study, but some things should not be rushed. Sometimes the best way to learn something is to take care and be methodical, and then steadily increase the pace of your practice.

In order to prepare for performance, you should push the pace in practice and make yourself uncomfortable. ***It is absolutely necessary to learn how to be comfortable with being uncomfortable*** if you want to perform at a level of excellence. It is important to practice a fast pace and quick tempo, but do not hurry your preparation.

THE "STEP UP" HAPPENS EVERY DAY

A lot of athletes say they will "step up their game" when they play their division rivals or that they will "step it up" in the big game. As a peak performance coach, this is both perplexing and insightful. It is perplexing because if you have the ability to "step up," why are you not "stepping up" at today's practice? It is simultaneously insightful because it shows the mentality of the player[s] saying this, illustrating an immature perspective towards performance. These players obviously do not understand the value of excellent preparation.

There is no "step up." If you can play at the highest level by stepping up, the step up must occur every day so that there is no step up. There is no conceivable reason to not play at your best during competition; there isn't even a conceivable reason to not do it in practice. As Michael Jordan said, "I play to win, whether during practice or a real game, and I will not let anything get in the way of me and my competitive enthusiasm to win." As His Airness would probably ask, why "step up" in the big game when it is what you should be doing every day in practice?

As we have discussed, performance reflects preparation. You will not maximize your potential if you pursue excellence only once in a while during practice sessions. If you wish to be a success, you must pursue excellence all the time. The "step up" happens every day. *Excellence is a lifestyle, not an event.*

MEASUREMENT = MOTIVATION

Dave Serrano, the head baseball coach at University of California, Irvine from 2005-2007 and the current head baseball coach at the University of Tennessee, is a true Master of the Mental Game. As head coach of the UCI Anteaters, Coach Serrano implemented mental conditioning as the foundation of the program. One of the keys to Coach Serrano's success with his team was his understanding that measurement equals motivation.

The best way to motivate yourself is to measure your progress. Simply believing that you will give your best without specific measurement of performance is unrealistic. Coach Serrano recognizes this and, with his attention to detail, he measures all the preparation of his team to motivate his players and to instill mental conditioning techniques. His simple utilization of a stopwatch is all it takes. By recording anything from the times running out of the batter's box to first base after a hit to the team's transitions from one drill to another, Coach Serrano gives his team measurements to gauge their daily efforts compared to their best times on record. In doing so, players on the team are held accountable for their efforts in their daily preparation, which makes the whole team practice harder and at a higher level on a consistent basis.

THE POWER OF TIME

During preparation, a stopwatch or video camera is the best accountability partner for a peak performer. The stopwatch is simple to use, unbiased, and blatantly honest about your performance effort. As the last section espoused, measurement equals motivation, and time is one of the great motivators in life. The utilization of a stopwatch is sure to motivate you to constantly improve your times, wherever appropriate, during your preparation routines

The use of a stopwatch anywhere, from lifting weights to simulating competitive game time scenarios, will draw the excellence out of your performance. By pressuring players to accomplish game-like scenarios in a limited amount of time, if not a shorter time than in during competition, they will learn to cope with uncomfortable situations. This can be applied to football by timing how long it takes for the offense to call a play, get to the line of scrimmage and snap the ball, or for increasing the efficiency and speed of getting the field goal team on the field at a moment's notice in game-like conditions. Ultimately, this forces players to work faster than they normally would if there were no stopwatch, and as fast or faster than they will need to be in a game.

Utilizing a stopwatch in your performance preparation will immediately increase the game-like speed, intensity, and tempo while you practice. You will also learn to cope with pressure and feel comfortable with uncomfortable situations, because on the edge of discomfort is where learning takes place.

Think about how you can implement a stopwatch in your preparation to help create an environment of pressure and discomfort to enhance your performance development. By keeping track of time and pushing yourself, the game will reward you for your efforts in your competitive performance.

CAIN'S CHALK TALK:
What can you measure to make your preparation process more competitive and to make you work faster than you might have to in a game?

1) _____

2) _____

3) _____

RECORD PROGRESS

One of the most effective methods to measure performance improvement is to regularly record your progress in a peak performance journal. When athletes take the initiative to record the details of their progress in a journal of some kind, they hold themselves accountable for their preparation. Such a journal can be used to keep quantifiable measurements of preparation drills, to help remove the emotions from daily preparation and to record factual assessments. Journaling can also can also be used to record reflections of daily performance, helping to understand how your feelings that day impacted your performance.

For each day of performance preparation, write down times, important lessons, areas in need of improvement, a goal for the next day based off today's practice session, and anything else that applies to your performance. Recording progress grants the opportunity to apply the three steps of performance improvement. It enables you to reflect on the information you record, generates awareness of areas of improvement, and enables you to create and implement new strategies for performance development. When you know what giving your best is and it is on record, you can better judge your effort with objectivity. This speeds up the learning and the improvement process. In sum, when you record progress, you make record progress.

HOW TO KEEP A PEAK PERFORMANCE FOOTBALL JOURNAL

One of the most beneficial routine exercises someone in the pursuit of excellence can do is keep a peak performance journal. The peak performance journal is a tool to help you further develop your mental skills for peak performance. Remember, you must be in control of yourself before you can control your performance. The first step in gaining self-control is to develop an awareness of your performance, so that you can recognize when you are distracted from the present moment and the most appropriate mental state for success.

DEVELOP AWARENESS

Developing awareness is the first step towards consistent levels of performance. Remember the three steps to performance change: (1) Awareness, (2) Strategy, (3) Implementation of the strategy. This journal provides you with an opportunity to record the different strategies you are working on to maintain and regain self-control.

GET IT OUT OF YOUR HEAD AND ON PAPER

The long-range goal is to develop various strategies you can implement in stressful situations to help you perform at your best when it means the most. If you choose to, the journal also can be a place where you can record your feelings and the personal knowledge that you are gaining about yourself, the game, your teammates, and any other factors. This is one of the few times in your life that you will ever direct so much energy toward one specific goal. There is a lot to learn from your pursuit of excellence. This journal will give you something to reflect on after your high-level participation is completed.

The journal also can serve as a place where you can express your feelings in writing or drawings. It is beneficial to get these feelings out in some way so that they do not build up and lead to unproductive tension. The use of colored pens is often helpful to express yourself, even if you are not an artist. Research has shown this strategy to be a beneficial stress management technique.

CREATE A ROUTINE FOR WRITING

You do not have to make an entry every day, but should strive to be consistent in your writing routine. **Remember, to be consistently successful you must be able to describe what you do as a process/routine.** Make your journal entries as routine as possible by writing at the same time of day or in a smipleplace, such as your locker, at the field or in your bed at home.

The journal is an informal record of your thoughts and experiences as you train for high-level performance. If you choose to have someone read your journal, please feel free to delete or cover up any parts that you think are too personal to share. The objective for someone who is reviewing your writing should be to guide you and to make suggestions that may facilitate your self-exploration in reaching your goals.

I highly recommend that you try the peak performance football journal as a strategy to learn about yourself and speed up your learning curve. Remember, it's the start that stops most people, so commit to it for the next 2-3 weeks and feel free to write whatever comes to your mind. The following section includes suggestions with accompanying questions/descriptors that can help guide your entries. As with all things, you will become more comfortable with the journal process as you develop a routine over time.

SAMPLE QUESTIONS TO WRITE ABOUT

1. **Peak Performance:** What does it feel like when you play and/or practice at your best? Describe some of your most enjoyable experiences playing football. What have you learned from these moments when you are playing at your best?

2. **Stressors:** Write down your thoughts about various events outside football that are distracting to you. For example, parents, girlfriends, peers, job hassles, financial issues, community (hometown expectations). Do the same for distractions on the field, such as importance of contest, location, spectators, etc.

3. **Coaching Style:** What do you need from your coaches? How can you best help them help you reach your goals? What can you

do to make your relationship with your coaches more productive?

4. **Teammates:** What do you want from your teammates? What can you give them? How do you relate and work with your teammates? Write about your relationship with other teammates. Any unfinished business you need to work through?

5. **Confidence:** At this time, how confident are you in regard to achieving your goals? What can you do differently to act more confidently? What can you ask of yourself, coach and/or teammates?

6. **Manifestations of Your Stress**: How do you experience high levels of anxiety in performance? Assess your thoughts, physiological and behavioral reactions. What strategies did you use to help intervene with your stress and keep balance?

7. **Awareness and Concentration:** What changes do you observe in your performance when you are aware? What concentration methods are you experimenting with? What are your ABC's or focal points for various skills?

TRUST YOUR PREPARATION

Football is the ultimate game of preparation. There is no other team sport where you will practice at least 4 times more than you play – and that doesn't even take off-season workouts, meetings, film sessions and in-season workouts into consideration! Tom Osborne of the University of Nebraska believed that 75% of the games were won or lost before the first practice even took place in the fall!

Therefore, preparation is everything to a football player. It is taking all the elements necessary for performance excellence and practicing them tirelessly and with a relentless energy to achieve progress. As you read through this book, integrate all the material into your preparation. The constant practice of mental conditioning with your physical conditioning is of utmost significance to reaching the pinnacle of performance excellence. As the great master of preparation, Coach John Wooden, used to say, "Failing to prepare is preparing to fail."

Most importantly, trust your preparation. Placing trust in your performance preparation and taking pride in the fact that you are doing things the right way will make all the difference in your journey. The climb up The Mountain of Excellence will undoubtedly be treacherous at times, but if you trust that you have prepared at a consistent effort of excellence, your preparation is bound to reward you.

CHAPTER #5 REVIEW

- ☐ "Nothing is better for intense game pressure than countless hours of disciplined effort spent mastering the fundamentals." – Coach John Wooden

- ☐ Repetition alone does not bring rewards; it is the quality that matters.

- ☐ Rewarded behavior becomes repeated behavior.

- ☐ Make practices competitive.

- ☐ Utilize a process-based scoring system to reward desired performance.

- ☐ Extra efforts give you the competitive advantage.

- ☐ Practice does not make perfect; practice makes permanent.

- ☐ Attention to details makes the difference.

- ☐ "Be quick, but do not hurry." – Coach John Wooden

- ☐ You must learn to be comfortable with being uncomfortable.

- ☐ The "step up" happens every day.

- ☐ Measurement equals motivation; you treasure what you measure.

- ☐ A stopwatch is a great motivator and accountability partner.

- ☐ When you record progress, you make record progress.
- ☐ "Failing to prepare is preparing to fail." – Coach John Wooden

CHAPTER #6

PERFORMANCE ROUTINES HOW YOU PLAY ONE PLAY AT A TIME

> "What is difficult becomes habitual, what is habitual becomes easy, what is easy is beautiful."
>
> **Constantin Stanislavski**
> **Inventor of "Method Acting"**

The secrets of success are hidden in the routines of our daily lives. You can know all the information within the previous chapters, but if you do not implement this information, then what good does it do for you? The purpose of any routine is to build more trust and consistency in performance.

Routines are effective because they give structure by providing a consistent starting point to activate a regular procedure. In football, a consistent frame of reference is essential to performance excellence by providing the mind and body a sense of security even under conditions that remain out of your control. The familiarity of routines establishes good performance habits, and your investment in cultivating them will pay big dividends on your pursuit of excellence.

This chapter will explore routines that will implement the information you learned in the previous chapters. This chapter will discuss routines that keep you in the present moment and focused on the process of playing one play at a time; routines that give you the necessary perspective to maintain a positive mentality; and routines to establish during your preparation, placing you in a position to give yourself the best chance for success.

PRE-GAME & POST-GAME ROUTINES

Pre-game and post-game routines are important for all coaches and players to develop. The purpose of these routines is to transform your mentality from your "real self" (boy scout) to your "performing self" (bounty hunter) and vice versa.

Most players have pre-game routines. Some individual pre-game routines I've witnessed range from players listening to a particular song or playlist, putting on their uniforms in a particular order, doing a certain set of stretches, and leaving the team to do mental imagery in silence for a couple minutes by themselves. Teams also have routines they follow before going out to perform in games, whether they are team warm-ups, team meetings/huddles, or team chants to bring up the energy levels. The purpose of these routines is to make you feel comfortable by giving you a sense of familiarity, which brings confidence, while transforming you into your competitive mentality.

Pre-game rituals are even more important to individuals and teams when you have to go on the road and play in an unfamiliar environment. Roger Barta, the head coach at Smith Center High School in Kansas from 1978-2012 and winner of 323 games and 8 state championships, knew this all too well. When his teams went on the road, they followed the same routine every time. Author Joe Drape described Barta's system in his book *Our Boys:* "After getting off the bus, the players walked directly onto the field and circled one goalpost, and then marched down to the other end of the field to do the same. This was part of the Redmen's pre-game ritual. It didn't matter that they were far away from home and on enemy ground; once the ball was kicked off, they would own this field. When the lap was completed, they returned to the bus to unload their equipment." ***Barta's routine helped his players find comfort in an uncomfortable environment.***

Post-game routines are a system of steps that allow the coaches and players to decompress after competition. Most players' post-game routines consist of having a brief post-game meeting with their coach or team, taking off their uniforms, cleaning themselves up, getting dressed, and calling it a day. Post-game routines, however, have the potential to be much more significant than this process of "going through the motions." Later in this chapter you'll learn how to create a post-game routine that enhances your pursuit of post-performance excellence so that you can extract as much learning as possible from each experience.

IN-GAME ROUTINES

An in-game routine provides the player and coach with a set of mental checkpoints. Kickers taking a certain number of steps, the quarterback calling the play the exact same way every time, and offensive linemen making pre-snap calls are just some of the many in-game routines performed in football. By going through a series of mental checkpoints, athletes place themselves in the present moment and focus on the process at hand. In the heat of competition, these routines serve as a chance for athletes to control themselves and their performances.

CAIN'S COACHING POINT:
The most important part of your pre-snap routine in football is that you take a deep breath. Taking a deep breath before the snap as a part of your pre-snap routine helps you to separate this play from other plays; it keeps you in the moment and in control of yourself.

THIS IS THE NUMBER ONE, MOST IMPORTANT PART OF THIS ENTIRE BOOK AS IT RELATES TO ON-FIELD PERFORMANCE AND PLAYING ONE PLAY AT A TIME!!! YES, THIS IS ALL CAPS... AND YES, I AM SCREAMING AT YOU!

Make sure that your coaches and teammates are aware of your in-game routines. This is important because they can act as accountability partners during performance and can remind you to check back into your routines if you are in a funk. You should also learn the in-game routines of your teammates so you can return their focus on a familiar frame of reference. In-game routines are imperative to self-control, giving you the best opportunity to execute with performance excellence.

CIRCLE OF FOCUS

Inside of your in-competition routine, you step into your circle of focus. The circle of focus is an imaginary circle that you step into and engage in a present-moment focus with your energy and attention going out towards the action taking place. For example, the offensive players step into their circle of focus as the quarterback calls out the cadence; the receiving team steps into its circle of focus as the official blows the whistle and makes the ball ready for play. Stepping into this metaphorical circle of focus is a critical part of the in-competition routine in which you get into the present moment and playing one play at a time.

As part of the in-competition routine, you want to use one to three mental strategies to keep your focus locked into the present.

1. Deep breath on a focal point

2. Visualization/Mental Imagery of execution of the play

3. Verbalize – Self-Talk of Final Thought/ABC's

CAIN'S COACHING POINT:
Because we cannot see if the athlete is doing mental imagery and we cannot see if he is using his final thought, as coaches, we want our athletes to take a deep breath each play so we can see that they are in control of themselves.

These strategies will assist your focus on performing in the present moment. Routine use of one or more of the strategies will help you enter that circle of focus and gain control of your mind. Mind control leads to body control, which leads to skill/performance control, and being in control of all aspects of yourself gives you the best chance for performance excellence.

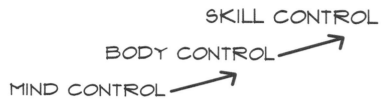

VERBALIZING YOUR FINAL THOUGHT

We have discussed how athletes use self-talk during performance, and an athlete's final thought builds upon the self-talk concept in a more play-specific manner. As discussed earlier, the final thought is the last thought in an athlete's mind before performing a specific aspect of the game. Before making a play, you want to think to yourself a particular positive phrase that intensifies your focus on the accomplishment of that play. You want to integrate this final thought into your performance routine to strengthen the mind-body performance connection. Mentally conditioning a final thought will establish a routine rhythm to your performance, giving you the best opportunity for performance excellence on a consistent play-by-play basis.

Internally verbalizing your final thought is called your block thought, tackle thought, cover thought, etc. There is a significant difference between being on the field and telling yourself "First step and Drive! First step and Drive! First step and Drive!" versus "Don't get beat inside...I have to make this block." Your final thought will make a big difference in your performance because a positive and aggressive final thought will give you the best chance to follow through in your performance.

DRILLS FOR FINAL THOUGHTS

Practicing final thoughts is important to maximize their effectiveness on a routine basis. With the football teams I work with, I set up a basic drill for each position group and have the players verbalize their final fundamental thoughts out loud. I have the linebackers tell me their tackle thought out loud, and I listen as well as watch the physical execution of the drill. Out loud, they are saying their final thought of "Eyes up! Come to balance! Eyes up! Come to balance!" They complete the drill and make the tackle. We take three reps with the verbalization of the final thought so that I can hear what their final thought is and see them using it with the rhythm of their body. *Their final thought is always one of their ABC's for performance as mentioned earlier in this book.*

If you know a teammate's final thought, then give him positive encouragement during the game. If his tackle thought is "Eyes up, come to balance," then you might say, "Let's keep our eyes up and come to balance right here!" after a missed tackle to help that player refocus on his final thought.

Peak performers also utilize mental imagery as a component of their performance routines. The use of mental imagery is an excellent way to psychologically prepare yourself for performance by visualizing yourself executing a specific performance task within your sport.

SUPERMAN SEGMENTATION AND SEPARATION

Segmentation routines are used to help separate yourself from the many different hats you wear. If you are reading this and you are a college or high school athlete, you have school, social activities, and sport to separate in your life; if you are a professional, you have at least the latter two. Inside of those different aspects of your life, you may wear the hat of son, brother, dad, significant other, friend, etc. One of the best techniques to help segment and separate the many hats you wear is to use something physical (perhaps a helmet!) to help you change your mental state. It is here we look to Superman for guidance.

Superman is the ultimate pro at segmentation and separation prior to and after his performances. He walks into the phone booth as Clark Kent, super nerd (student), and comes out as Superman (football player and one-play warrior), superhero. His self-transformative process is the perfect example for peak performance segmentation routines. The nearest phone booth is the symbolic equivalent of his locker room: As he changes his clothes, his perspective changes, as he adopts a peak performance mentality.

One football team I worked with took this principle so far as to get a Superman logo for the outside of their locker room door to serve as a reminder that when you walked into the locker room to change your clothes, you were also changing your mentality from student (Clark Kent) to athlete (Superman).

As you take off each item of your street clothes and put on that football uniform or T-shirt and shorts for conditioning, think about the transformation taking place and the necessary change in mentality. Release the mental bricks from your personal life as you get into your performance mentality, or release the mental bricks of your performance after practice as you return yourself to your personal life. Changing your clothes is a process to help you separate the mentality you need to succeed in the various segments of your life, by breaking down the process into various segments. The establishment of these routines gives you the best chance to be in the present for whatever you are about to perform, and to have a consistent mentality to be where you need to be when you need to be there.

MOVE THROUGH THE HOURGLASS

 Another way to think about the process of routines, segmentation and separation is to imagine an hourglass as a visual example of how your pre-performance and post-performance routines will work. The shape of the hourglass reflects the segmentation and separation process, with a definite start point (top of the hourglass) and end point (bottom of the hourglass) with a defined middle section.

This hourglass shape mirrors the self-transformative routine because you begin the process as either your "real self" or "performing self" and end as the opposite. The hourglass transformation is marked by some physical routine actions such as changing clothes, where you strip down from your school clothes to your team uniform. When you are naked during the process of changing, you are in the middle of that transformative process — the middle of the hourglass.

Changing your clothes is common routine for segmentation and separation; but a number of other routines, such as turning off the cell phone, buckling up your chin strap or taking a shower, can also mark the self-transformation.

 CAIN'S COACHING POINT:
I suggest using your cell phone as a tool to help you transform yourself and as a reminder to stay in the present moment. When you turn off your cell phone, it is a sign that you are shifting your mentality from student to athlete, and that you are letting go of the academics, social media, significant other, friends, family and other potential distractions that could keep you from being the ultimate athlete. When you turn off that cell phone, you are going to feel yourself moving through your mental hourglass and becoming a peak performer.

The athletes I work with hardly ever turn their cell phones off, so when they do, that means they are going to be doing something special. You have got to treat practice and games like they are special opportunities for development, because they are. Let nothing outside of your sport interfere with mentally preparing for performance.

CAIN'S COACHING POINT:
If you are a coach, I suggest you get practice uniforms for your team, something as simple as the same T-shirt and/or shorts. This will help your athletes with the segmentation process as they change into a uniform. You will teach them the importance of the mindset that they need to have when that uniform is on. Invest the time to educate them on the importance of changing the clothes and changing the mindset to get present.

After you turn your cell phone off, you then start the process of changing your clothes. As you take off your shirt, let go of the test you failed. As you take off your pants, let go of the person who cut you off on your drive into practice. As you take off your shoes, there go the issues you are having at home. As you physically change your clothes, you are ridding yourself of all that mental baggage and turning yourself into the ultimate athlete. As you move toward the middle of the hourglass, you become fully present and fully focused on what you plan to accomplish today at practice.

Then, as you put on your performance gear, you feel yourself getting more energized and more focused. As you lace up your spikes, you feel locked in and prepared to perform to the best of your abilities, striving for performance excellence. Finally, you come out on the other end of the hourglass, mentally prepared to DOMINATE THE DAY! By following this hourglass segmentation and separation routine, you are setting the stage for a quality performance.

NORTH COUNTRY UNION TRACK RULE

Bob Davis is the former head football coach at North Country Union High School in Newport, VT. During his tenure, Davis' teams won three state championships and he was named Vermont coach of the year three times. When I worked with him in 2004, he developed his so-called "track rule." He instructed his players that when they crossed the cinder track that ringed the football field the only thing that mattered was North Country Football. He coached his players to use the track as the last bit of their routine to help segment between their student/social self (real self) and their football self (performing self). What is your metaphorical track at your football facility?

WHEN IS THE GLADIATOR READY FOR BATTLE?

 The last thing you do before performance should be part of a physical routine to signal you are ready to perform. One of the best illustrations of this is in the movie *Gladiator,* when Maximus (Russell Crowe) reaches down for a bit of earth to rub between his hands and then throws the remnants back to the ground. This is his pre-game routine symbolizing he has gathered his battle mentality. It is a sign that Maximus is in the present moment, nothing can distract his focus, and he is ready to perform in war.

Develop your own pre-game routine to collect your performance mentality. I often suggest that you take a moment and retie your spikes to check into your performance state of mind. By doing this, you lace it up and lock it in. NBA superstar LeBron James powders his hands and tosses the remnants in the air, in an act similar to that of Maximus. Whatever the physical act may be, use it to activate your performance mentality and enter your circle of focus. Let yourself know that you are Gladiator ready and going to battle on the gridiron as a one-play warrior.

FOCAL POINTS, DEEP BREATHS, SELF-CONTROL

Whenever you perform, it is important to have and utilize focal points. Focal points are mental checkpoints that you go to throughout your journey up The Mountain of Excellence as a part of your in-competition routine. You check in on your mental and emotional state and, when necessary, bring yourself back into the present moment. Football players could use a spot on the scoreboard or somewhere in the stadium as a focal point that they go to and take a deep breath between plays or when the game starts to speed up on them. Russell Wilson spoke about using a focal point to help him slow down and stay in control with the emotions of playing in Super Bowl XLVIII. This technique allows players to have a routine in which they are able to look at their focal point, take a deep breath and get back to a calm, focused and centered place in the present moment ready for the next play. **Remember, you must be in control of yourself before you can control your performance, and the #1 way to get control of yourself is to take a deep breath.**

The routine use of a focal point and a deep breath will put you in control of yourself and in a better place mentally and physically, giving you the best chance for success.

CAIN'S CHALK TALK:
What is a focal point you can use at your practice field to help you regain control?

_____

_____

TAKE A DEEP BREATH

The deep breath is an important part of any performance routine, because the breath connects you to the present moment. Taking a deep breath pulls you right back to the "here" and the "now." The deep breath brings oxygen into your system, slows down your heart rate, clears your mental state and puts you back in control of yourself.

CAIN'S CHALK TALK:
When as a part of your pre-snap routine can you take a deep breath?

_____

_____

As a football coach, you want to see your players breathe between each play so that you have a visual reference point to identify where your players are at mentally each play. Having them take a deep breath enables you as the coach to recognize when players are letting the game speed up on them and if they are working a process to help them settle back down and stay in control of their emotions. In pressure situations, often the first thing to break down will be the player's routine. Once a player loses his routine, next goes his mind control, then his physical performance. Make sure to take your deep breaths during performance to keep your head in YOUR game.

ROUTINE PERFORMANCE REVIEW

A routine review of your most recent performance is one of the best post-game routines you can establish on your pursuit of performance excellence. Keeping a peak performance journal chronicles your progress and development in your mental and physical conditioning, providing you with a valuable resource for self-improvement. This gives you the ability to reflect upon past performances and recall how you performed, how you were feeling, what you believe you need to improve, what performance adjustments you must make, whether or not past performance adjustments worked, etc. In the previous chapter I addressed how recorded progress becomes record progress, and making the act of recording performances a routine is the first step in the right direction.

The best time to integrate this performance routine review is directly after performance, while it is fresh in your mind. Record all the information about your performance that is applicable to future improvement. As you push yourself to excellence, challenge yourself to become better by being self-critical and not being merely content with a solid performance. Make sure, however, that you also give some focus to what you did well. Doing this will serve as a reminder to you to continue performing these aspects of the game and will enable you to catch yourself if those aspects of your game start slipping. This is all invaluable information for developing your performance to become a peak performer in football.

"Our practice schedule at Tech was the same throughout the season. The periods on Tuesday were the same every single Tuesday. Wednesday was the same every week, etc. Our schedules were very regular, so everyone knew what was expected of them. It gave the guys one less thing to worry about, and it helped us monitor progress more easily. Going about it this way allowed us to have a consistent level of skill development."

Mike Leach
Head Football Coach
Washington State University

MAKE IT ROUTINE

"A routine is a skill that needs to be practiced regularly so that it becomes, well, routine. You cannot just do a routine once and expect to have it show up for you in the heat of the competitive arena known as football. The routine has to be something you do on a daily basis in practice. Game-like practice is critical to your mental game development because it enhances your ability to stick to your routines in pressure situations. Ultimately, the purpose of routines is to provide something physical to assist us with something mental.

Remember, practice makes permanent. You want to drill these routines during your preparation, making them such a permanent part of your performance process that you unconsciously tune into a predetermined mindset for performance excellence. It is also worth noting that you should approach your routine in the same manner you approach the entire performance - with quality effort, attention to detail, and present-moment focus on the process.

Breaking down all elements of your performance into routines will ultimately make it a routine performance and give you the structure that will enable you to develop performance excellence and play one play at a time. Making performance skills routine ultimately makes the experience of climbing The Mountain of Excellence feel much simpler and gives you a tremendous boost of confidence.

CHAPTER #6 REVIEW

☐ The secrets of success are hidden in the routines of our daily lives.

☐ Pre-game and post-game routines are important to get yourself into and out of your performance mentality.

☐ In-game routines enhance self-control.

☐ Step into your circle of focus during performance.

☐ Establish a final thought for performance tasks.

☐ Superman used segmentation and separation techniques, and so should you.

☐ Move through the hourglass for performance self-transformation.

☐ Lace it up and lock it in to be Gladiator ready.

☐ During performance, use focal points to mentally check in.

☐ Integrate taking a deep breath into your performance routines.

☐ Performance routines must be regularly practiced to maximize their potentials.

CHAPTER #7

RECOGNIZE, RELEASE, REFOCUS

> "Our job is just to play, go out there, and have fun. We need to drop this rucksack we're carrying around that's weighing us down – the expectations – and relax and play the game."
>
> **Rich Ellerson**
> **Former Head Football Coach**
> **United States Military Academy**

Recognizing your physical, emotional and mental state within the context of your competitive environment is critical to staying in control of yourself, thereby giving yourself the best opportunity for success.

The development of a routine in which you recognize where you are at mentally, emotionally and physically and where you have a release to use when you are in a negative place so that you can refocus on the next play is an essential part of playing football one play at a time.

This chapter will give you the skills to develop your own one-play-at-a-time mental management system to keep your state of mind active and engaged in the moment as you journey up The Mountain of Excellence.

RECOGNIZING YOUR SIGNAL LIGHTS

The most challenging aspect of the mental game is learning to recognize when your performance is taking a turn for the worse and then developing a system to make the necessary corrections to return to a place of performance excellence.

The recognition that you are having a performance breakdown is the primary and most crucial step in the process of playing one play at a time. Recognizing where you are – mentally, emotionally, and physically – is called your Awareness To Win (#ATW). Nobody is perfect. All football coaches and players lose control of themselves on occasion, but it is the performer who can correct himself the quickest who tends to perform consistently and, ultimately, has more success.

SIGNAL LIGHTS FOR FOOTBALL EXPLAINED

If you are driving a car and you come to a green light, you would naturally GO! If you are driving a car and the light turns yellow, some of us would slow down while others would speed up, depending on where we are in relation to the light. When you come to a red light, however, you must stop or you are going to crash and burn. Now, if you are reading this chuckling to yourself about the time you ran a red light and didn't cause an accident or get caught by the police, then I am with you. However, we must caution against such consistent action - because you might run a red light once and live, but do it routinely and you will crash and burn.

OFFICER CAIN'S COACHING POINT:
"Be aware of your signal lights in football. If you run through red lights, you will crash and burn. Play as many plays as you can in green lights to give yourself the best chance for success."

Performance awareness in football is similar to driving a car on the road. When you have green lights (positive, confident, specific, and aggressive thoughts and feelings), you are in control of yourself. In performance, you encounter yellow lights (hopeful, uncertain, vague, and timid thoughts and feelings), which occur when something negative happens to take you out of a green light mentality. If your yellow lights are not recognized and addressed, then you will often find yourself in red lights (negative, dejected, apathetic, and destructive thoughts and feelings). Playing in yellow or red lights is a recipe for beating yourself with a poor performance.

The easiest way for you to think about your signal lights is this:

Green – You are giving yourself the best opportunity for performance excellence.

Yellow – You are starting to lose the mentality conducive to peak performance.

Red – You are totally out of control and it is reflecting in your performance.

The goal of all peak performers is to play the game of football with green lights as much as possible, while focusing on the next 30 feet of the journey.

CAUSES OF YELLOW & RED LIGHTS

One thing that makes football such a unique and special game is its physical nature. It is this inherent violence that draws so many of us to the sport, because it provides a tremendous rush of adrenaline like no other prior to the game. The violence, however, creates fear. Former all-pro offensive lineman Dave Szott felt this way: "The great thing about football is you have to face your fear. Any player that ever played this game has felt fear, and if they say no, they're lying." Nothing will remove you from your green light mentality faster than fear, and that's just before the game! When competition begins, yellow and red lights could result from making a mistake, an official making a bad call, a coach's criticism, fans getting on your nerves, your opponent talking trash, or any number of other things that can become stuck in your head.

Adversity comes in all forms, physical and mental, and does not have to involve events within your performance environment. The world outside of your performance arena also can affect your performance if you are not in control of yourself. These might include that grudge against your boss, the schoolwork you must accomplish or your latest love interest. Do not let these things distract you from your present-moment focus and peak performance mentality of competing one play at a time. Focusing on what you are trying to avoid, instead of what you are trying to accomplish, is a recipe for disastrous performance and a signal that you are in a yellow or red light.

GREEN LIGHT LESSONS FROM SOUTH BEND

Linebacker Ned Bolcar was part of the renaissance of the Notre

Dame football program in the 1980's. The team hit rock bottom in 1985, including a 58-7 humiliation at the hands of archrival Miami. The turnaround of the program that culminated in the 1988 national championship began with ATTITUDE, according to Bolcar. He illustrated the point by telling a story about the 1986 game with Michigan.

"We had this routine we did. We would line up across the 20-yard line and run plays into the end zone. When our warm-ups ended, we would punt out of the end zone and go into the tunnel. Well, Michigan had to go in through the same tunnel. But instead of running down the sideline, they decided to run right through our drills. If Michigan did this to us the year before, we'd probably have just watched them run through our drills. This time, a big offensive lineman named Tom Rehder stuck out his arm and clotheslined a Michigan player named John Kolesar. Then another player grabbed Tom and a little fight broke out. Was this our fault? No. Michigan made a decision. They wanted to test us. And we laid down the law: This is our stadium, our field, and nobody comes in here and pushes us around. We're not taking anything from anyone."

It was clear to the opponents, fans and anyone else in the stadium that this Notre Dame team was IN GREEN LIGHTS – they were confident, aggressive and focused on what they could control! In football, if your mind is illuminated by the red lights of a negative mentality, you are nearly guaranteed to be on the losing end of your competition. Focusing on what you are trying to avoid instead of what you are trying to accomplish is a recipe for disastrous performance in football and in life.

THREE WAYS TO RECOGNIZE YOUR SIGNAL LIGHTS

There are three major areas in which you can develop your performance awareness and learn to better recognize your signal lights. The three areas in which you can often recognize where you are at mentally, physically, and emotionally are these:

1. Self-talk – What you are saying to yourself

2. Physical feelings – How you are feeling, physically

3. Situations – Circumstances which arise in performance that will trigger particular signal lights

CAIN'S COACHING POINT:
The purpose of routines is to maintain self-control and get into a green light performance mentality as often as possible.

GREEN LIGHTS – THE CAT MENTALITY

Green lights are an easy concept to comprehend. They represent the mentality of peak performance; where you are feeling positive, aggressive, and confident; focused on the present process at hand; and in control of your performance thoughts and actions. Green lights are performance movers and confidence builders. One football player I worked with referred to the green light mentality as the CAT mentality – Confident, Aggressive and Tough.

When you are confident, aggressive and tough, you are locked into the moment and moving forward with green lights. Staying in the green light zone, you give yourself the best opportunity to have an excellent performance on this play.

In order to recognize when you are not in a green light state of mind, you must first recognize what signs indicate that you are in the green. The next three sections will help you use the three major areas of signal light recognition to identify your green light mentality.

GREEN LIGHTS – SELF-TALK

When you have green lights, what are you saying to yourself? Some examples could be:

1. You cannot touch me - bring it!

2. I am feeling it, so they better bring it.

3. I own this field; this is my house.

4. Yes sir, I am too good.

Green light thoughts are much like your confidence conditioning statements, but they are shorter and very specific to your athletic performance. They are usually aggressive, external, specific and confident thoughts.

CAIN'S CHALK TALK:
Write down your green light thoughts – what do you say to yourself when you are playing at your best?

_____

_____

GREEN LIGHTS – PHYSICAL FEELINGS

When you have green lights, how do you feel physically? Most football players report:

1. I feel light on my feet.

2. My muscles are relaxed and I have good energy.

3. I feel strong and I have big body language.

CAIN'S CHALK TALK:
Write down your green light feelings – how do you feel about yourself when you are playing at your best?

_____

_____

GREEN LIGHT - SITUATIONS

What situations or actions in competition, practice, the weight room or academic settings put you into green lights?

Most football players report:

1. When I have a great warm-up

2. When I have had a good night's sleep

3. When I practiced my presentation over and over, so I knew the content forward and backward

4. When I stick with my routine

CAIN'S CHALK TALK:
Write down the situations in performance that will place you into your green light – the situations where you know you will play at your best.

_____

_____

RED & YELLOW LIGHTS

Football players I have worked with in the past have occasionally become caught up in trying to identify whether they were in a red light or yellow light. As an athlete, I want you not to get hung up on that distinction because it is counterproductive to peak performance. This distinction is more relevant for coaches because they must discern which measure will help you get back into your green light mentality – coaching you on taking a deep breath, calling a timeout or making a substitution.

As an athlete, the distinction does not matter as much. Red lights are negative thoughts, confidence cutters, and performance stoppers

- and yellow leads you there. Green is where you want to be. All you need to identify is whether or not you are giving yourself the green light. If you are not in the green, then recognize, release and refocus on the performance at hand. The next three sections will help you use the three major areas of signal light recognition to identify whether you are in red/yellow lights.

RED/YELLOW/LIGHTS – SELF-TALK

When you have red/yellow lights, what are you saying to yourself?

Most football players report:

1. I cannot believe the official made that call.

2. Why is coach saying that?

3. Why can't I catch anything?

4. Why do I play this stupid game?

5. I suck.

CAIN'S CHALK TALK:
Write down your red/yellow light thoughts – what do you say to yourself when you are struggling on the field?

_____

_____

RED/YELLOW LIGHTS – PHYSICAL FEELINGS

When you have red/yellow lights, how do you feel physically?

Most football players report:

1. I do not feel good; I feel tired and slow.

2. I feel like I cannot catch my breath.

3. My equipment feels heavy.

4. The ball feels like a foreign object.

5. I feel like the game's speeding up on me.

CAIN'S CHALK TALK:
Write down your red/yellow light feelings – what do you feel physically when you are struggling on the field?

_____

_____

RED /YELLOW LIGHT - SITUATIONS

What situations or actions in competition, practice, the weight room or academic settings put you into red/yellow lights?

Most football players report:

1. When I fail to execute a play

2. When an official makes bad call

3. When a teammate makes a potentially costly error

4. When I know I could have prepared better

CAIN'S CHALK TALK:
Write down what situations in performance will put you into a red/yellow light and what happens when you are playing at your worst. What removes you from your green light mentality?

_____

SIGNAL LIGHTS = PERFORMANCE CHANGE

Once you have identified your self-talk, your physical feelings and the situations that put you into your green and red/yellow lights, you immediately give yourself a better chance to recognize your signal lights in performance. If you have green lights, refocus on the next play. If you have red/yellow lights, you must release before you refocus.

Remember the three steps to performance change:

1. Develop awareness of what needs to change.

2. Develop a strategy for change to happen.

3. Put that strategy into action.

Most athletes do not know how to make necessary performance adjustments because they have not developed performance awareness. Performance change is all about understanding your internal signal lights. **Mentally, what you are aware of you can control; what you are unaware of is going to control you.** This is why understanding and practicing the signal lights concept gives you the best opportunity to effectively exercise the three steps of performance change.

INVERTED U OF SIGNAL LIGHTS

Peak Performance 101 is about understanding the Inverted U.

On the North-South axis we have performance, and on the East-West axis there is intensity or focus.

How excited are you?

When you are not intense or focused enough, performance is low. Conversely, when you are overly intense or are too focused and trying too hard, performance is still low. This is why it is important for peak performers to maintain a consistent mental state of excellence to compete with optimal energy and perform at their best on a consistent play-to-play basis. The pre-snap routine and, most importantly, your deep breath allow you to manage your mental, emotional and physical self to stay in the moment and at your peak of optimal energy on the Inverted U of Performance.

This mental state of performance excellence is maintained through the adoption of performance routines that create a mental management. A mental management routine takes you from falling just anywhere on the inverted U and gives you a much better chance of consistently falling in the center, which is your optimal energy and arousal area for a peak performance. This routine-based mental maintenance system gives you the best chance of performing at the peak of the Inverted U.

PERFORMANCE ROUTINES

Performance routines are the life jacket of peak performance. When the pressure is on, as it usually is in football, you turn to your routines so that you can stay in the present moment and increase your chances of achieving performance excellence on the next play. The importance of routines to performance is a simple formula: Routines lead to consistency, consistency leads to confidence, and confidence leads to success.

CAIN'S COACHING POINT:
To be consistent over time, you must be able to describe what you do as a process/routine.

The best football programs I have worked with as a mental conditioning coach have specific systems and structured performance routines that help players perform consistently over the course of the game and the season. These programs often stress the importance of having a focal point to turn to during pressure performances. When you get distracted or you have red/yellow light thoughts and start beating yourself up, your focal point is your box of positive thoughts - they represent your checkpoint to help you slow down and get back into your green lights.

RELEASE

Once you have learned to recognize your signal lights, the next step in the process is developing a release routine to help you rid yourself of the negative emotion that will slow you down.

The purpose of your release/physical routine is to help you get back in control of yourself and back into your green lights.

This release routine facilitates your transition back to a green light mentality. When you are in red/yellow lights, you must develop some sort of physical routine to help you mentally release the negative frustration. This physical action should be an expressive release to get control of your mental state and return you to the pursuit of performance excellence on the next play.

CAIN'S CHALK TALK:
Examples of common releases are to clap your hands, take a deep breath, or undo and redo part of your equipment such as a chin strap or gloves. What are physical releases you can use to help you get from

red/yellow lights and back to green?

_____

_____

RELEASE YOUR MENTAL BRICKS

At the beginning of this chapter, we read about the Army football players carrying around a "rucksack" of expectations that were prohibiting them from performing at their highest level. The reality is that at one point or another, we all make errors and mistakes or fall prey to unrealistic expectations. There is a common tendency to continue to carry these mistakes and poor performances with us, resulting in a buildup of negative mental energy. Instead of beating yourself up over a poor performance, you must learn to release these "mental bricks" that weigh on your mind.

If, every time you make a mistake, you were to grab a physical brick and carry that brick with you, it would weigh you down both physically and mentally. This would invariably inhibit you from performing to the best of your ability.

Now, visualize a mistake you are bitter about as a mental brick. When you carry this mistake with you, this mental brick, it takes the same toll as carrying a physical brick. The difference is you cannot see it because it is a weight within your mind.

In your quest for excellence, you must train yourself to release the mental bricks that threaten to weigh you down. Releasing your mental bricks relies on a process of reflection and realization followed by the release. After a mistake or a poor performance, you must thoughtfully reflect on the experience and consider how you can improve. Once you have realized what improvements can be made in your performance, you can then release the error from your consciousness and move on to the next play. The release process should happen in between snaps and happen as quickly as possible.

Releasing a negative play and getting to the next play is a skill that must be developed through repetition.

EXAMPLES OF IN-GAME RELEASES

In-game releases should be directed at a consistent focal point. Your focal point could be an object somewhere in the stadium or on a part of your equipment. Whatever that focal point may be, when you look at it, you should take a good deep breath, push out your chest, get big and put all of that red/yellow light, negative energy and self-doubt into that focal point and let it go.

As you transfer that energy, remind yourself to get back to the next play and what's important now (#WIN) and return to your green light thoughts and green light/refocus routine.

As a quarterback, you could unbutton your chin strap, take a deep breath, and button it up again. This physical action allows you to make a mental connection to the next play. Receivers can unfasten their gloves, find the focal point, take two deep breaths, then refasten the Velcro straps and clap twice. In the process, they get rid of the last play and can then refocus on the most important play of the game... the next one!

Some coaches want their players to all have the same release, such as slapping a thigh pad and taking a deep breath, so that they only have to watch for one release from everyone. Whether you have each player come up with his own, do it by position or have the entire team use the same release, that is up to you as the coach. Each release should have something physical that they do plus a deep breath.

Here are some more examples of release routines:

You can shake your hands to shake off the red/yellow light thoughts.

You can make a fist, and as you release your fingers, release the past play.

You can clap your hands together and move on to the next play.

You can spit the red/yellow lights away.

There are hundreds of different releases you can use. The important part of the release is to be sure that you have something physical that you do, and that you are taking a deep breath and have a focal point as a part of your release.

FLUSH IT

A fun way to think about releasing mental bricks is by conjuring the image of a toilet. When you have a mental brick that is in danger of putting you in red lights, you want to take this mental brick and "flush it." Once you are relieved of that mental brick, you are ready to return to the present moment in your performance.

University of Vermont Men's Hockey head coach Kevin Sneddon took this concept and integrated it into part of his team's post-performance routine. He keeps a miniature foam toilet in the team dressing room, and after a frustrating period or a hard-fought game, he and his players will flush the mental bricks from their performance.

"I ask each of my players to flush the game down the toilet and move on," says Coach Sneddon. "The visual works quite well."

It is inevitable, as you climb The Mountain of Excellence, that you will face forms of adversity that weigh on your mind. Do not carry these mental bricks with you on your journey. Stop routinely at your mental toilet to relieve yourself of their weight. Perform your release routine to flush away the negativity built within those mental bricks. Your mind will feel lighter and clearer, and you will be more mentally agile when you get back to your climb of playing the next play.

REFOCUS ON THE NEXT PLAY

Once you recognize your signal lights and release your red/yellow lights with your release routine, it becomes critical that you refocus back into the present moment and on the next play.

Refocusing returns your mind to the next play and pushes you towards performance excellence. One of the best ways you can refocus is to talk out loud with your teammates during competition. **When you talk out loud, you are external and present**. When you are quiet, you can easily get lost in your own head, thinking about the past or the future. Refocus back to the present moment - you will give yourself the best chance to perform at your best by talking out loud and being an energy giver.

SO WHAT, NEXT PLAY! MENTALITY

Let me ask you this. Are you that bad that every call and every bounce has to go your way to win? If the answer is no, why do you get so angry when an official makes a bad call or a play doesn't go your way?

Keep in mind that great plays are as much of a pitfall for players and coaches in terms of refocusing. It is critical that you flush away the excitement and thrill of the explosive play you just made – or that call from the sideline – and get in the moment as soon as possible.

Refocusing, just like all mental conditioning, requires that your mind and body work together. If your body is trying to play the game in the moment and your mind is still analyzing a previous play or thinking about the possibility of play in the future, your mind and body are working against each other and you lose.

You want to live in the big picture and compete in the moment. When things aren't going your way, you have got to embrace adversity. Say "So What, Next Play!" (#SWNP). Let go of the past, and get back to competing in the present moment and executing on the next play.

"So What, Next Play!" is a verbal key that you can use to help refocus you and your teammates back into the present moment. This key helps you bridge from the past by saying "So What" and returns you where you want to be in the present by saying "Next Play."

You cannot just say "So What, Next Play!" with your mouth; you have to say it with your body as well. By using your physical release routine to return to the present, regardless of how you feel about the past play, saying "So What, Next Play!" refocuses your mind. You can then actively engage in the most important part of your performance – the next 30 feet.

In life and sport, negative things happen. Adversity is going to strike and there is nothing you can do to stop it. And why would you want to stop adversity? Adversity is a positive. Adversity is what causes you to grow. Adversity and success are neighbors on the highway to excellence; you can't get one without the other.

Some tragedies are simply outside of your control. What you cannot do is allow yourself to get caught up in a moment that has already passed. You must constantly move on to the next play. This "So What, Next Play!" mentality is the hallmark of a peak performer on the gridiron.

REFOCUS SIGN

When I go on the bench of top football teams, I often hang up a sign that says "REFOCUS." I teach the players that when they recognize their minds starting to wander, they only have to look at the sign and refocus. Using the sign as a focal point gets them back into the next play. This is another very simple yet highly effective tool to help you get back into the present moment.

THE RECOGNIZE – RELEASE – REFOCUS CYCLE

The process of recognize-release-refocus is an important one to master in your pursuit of performance excellence in football. This process is founded on an internal awareness of your signal lights, especially the ability to recognize when you are out of your green light mentality. Upon recognizing your yellow or red light state of mind, you must make a present-moment performance change by performing your release routine in order to refocus for the next play.

This process is conceptually simple and highly effective, yet it is amazing how many athletes neglect this cycle to maximize their performance potential.

This is one of the mental conditioning systems that separates the good from the great performers. If you want to perform at a consistently high level of excellence, you must learn how to recognize your signal lights, release frustration from past plays, and refocus on the present moment in competition.

CAIN'S COACHING POINT:
When you have adversity and bad calls that go against you, use the verbal for release & refocus, which is "So What, Next Play!"

A REALISTIC LOOK AT "THE ZONE"

I do not think you will ever be in green lights for an entire game. If you find yourself in "the zone," with that relaxed intensity and your green lights on steady, then enjoy the ride, baby, 'cause it does not happen often!

It is an experience you may have once - maybe never. Over the careers of the greatest performers on the planet, this kind of "zone" may happen only a handful of times.

Peak performance is not about being in "the zone" all the time and having everything in the game go your way. Adversity is built into the fabric of football, making every competition unique and full of new variables and situations for players to overcome.

Peak performance is about playing your best when you need it the most, each and every play. It is about compensating and adjusting your performance to the present-moment conditions of performance. It is about handling and managing pressure better than the opposition. It is about rolling with the punches until you get the job done. The better your routines and the more systematic your approach, the better your chance to stay in the green lights and perform on the level of excellence one play at a time.

Great athletes embrace adversity. They welcome it and they starve for it, because they know their ability to overcome adversity is what makes them great. The more adverse the conditions that day for both teams, the better they play because they know they are better equipped to handle adversity than the opponent.

KNOW YOUR 4R CYCLE

You want to work on your release and refocus routines every day just like you do your stance and starts in football. It may only be for only two minutes. As part of your in-competition *Routine*, you want to work on your ability to *Recognize* your physical and mental state, *Release,* and *Refocus* on the next play every day in practice.

If you know what your red/yellow lights are and you fail to make a performance change by implementing release and refocus routines to return to your green light mentality, then you are not maximizing your performance potential. You are no better off than your competitor who has not invested the time to read this book and has not cultivated a deeper understanding of the mental game of football.

Knowing what to do but not doing what you know means you are no better off than the person who has no idea what to do. *Be a "Do-er," not a "Know-er."*

CHAPTER #7 REVIEW

☐ The ability to recognize your physical, emotional and mental state within the context of your competitive environment is absolutely necessary.

☐ Green signal lights – you are giving yourself the best opportunity for performance excellence.

☐ Yellow signal lights – you are starting to lose the mentality conducive to peak performance.

☐ Red signal lights – You are totally out of control and it is reflecting in your performance.

☐ Mastery of performance awareness is developed by understanding your self-talk, physical feelings, and how you deal with common situations during performance.

☐ A routine-based mental maintenance system keeps you at the peak of the Inverted U of Performance.

☐ To be consistent over time, you must be able to describe your routines as a process.

☐ The purpose of your release/physical routine is to help you get back in control of yourself and back into your green lights.

☐ Release your mental bricks.

☐ All releases should be directed at a consistent focal point.

☐ Be sure to take a deep breath during your release.

☐ When you have a mental brick, relieve your mind and "Flush It."

☐ Refocus on WIN (What's Important Now).

☐ Develop a "So What, Next Play!" mentality to refocus when adversity strikes.

☐ Use a refocus sign as a focal point.

☐ Peak performance is not about being in "the zone." It is about making the necessary adjustments to perform consistently at a level of excellence and to be able to compensate and adjust.

CHAPTER #8

RESPONSE-ABILITY

> "Some people believe in luck. If we did, why don't you put a rabbit's foot in your hat, rub a bald head, and win the game? We believe in hard work and being trained for that moment when your number's called. Some people don't believe that. I believe in competitive excellence. Why not just hope fate takes over?"
>
> *-Urban Meyer*
> *Head Football Coach*
> *Ohio State University*
> *2 national championships*

The most powerful ten-word sentence in the English language consists of only seven short two-letter words. That sentence is: **If it is to be, it is up to me.** This encapsulates response-ability.

Response-ability is taking ownership of your past, commanding your present and taking charge of your future. It is being accountable for your perspective and controlling how you choose to respond to adversity. Too many people are negatively affected by outside influences they cannot control. They respond by becoming a victim of outside factors, rather than responding to adversity by holding themselves responsible for their actions. *Choosing your response in any situation is the greatest of all personal powers we possess as human beings.*

In this chapter, the importance of response-ability will be made clear. You will learn how response-ability makes a difference in performance and how to begin disciplining your mind to respond to events in order to produce productive outcomes.

MAN FREEZES TO DEATH
LACK OF RESPONSE-ABILITY

In the February 1978 issue of *Success Unlimited*, psychologist Dr. Dudley Calvert tells the story of a railway employee in Russia who accidentally locked himself in a refrigerator car. Inside the car, he could not unlock the door nor could he attract the attention of those outside. Unable to escape, he resigned himself to his fate. As he felt his body becoming numb, he documented his story and his approaching death in sentences scribbled on the wall of the car.

"I am becoming colder now," he wrote. "Still colder, now I can hardly write..." and, finally, "these may be my last words." And they were.

When the car was opened upon arrival at its destination, other railway employees found him dead. Yet, the temperature of the car was 56 DEGREES! The freezing apparatus had been out of order in the car and was inaccurately stuck on 28 degrees. There was no physical reason for his death. There was plenty of air – he hadn't suffocated. What happened was he gave away his personal power and defeated himself by not responding appropriately to the challenges in front of him. He let the power of his mind negatively affect his reality. *Remember, perspective is reality and you are response-able for choosing any attitude and any perspective you want in any given situation.* His own lack of response-ability led to his demise, a victim of his own delusion.

MAN OVERCOMES HELL ON EARTH
RESPONSE-ABILITY

In *Man's Search for Meaning*, Viktor Frankl talks about his unfathomable experience and survival of the Nazi concentration camps in World War II. Frankl, a psychologist, knew he was response-able for his mental state and only chance at survival in his hell-on-earth conditions. He chose to search for something of value and meaning every day of his struggle.

Living in the concentration camp, Frankl discovered the Nazis could take away his family, his freedom, his food and health, but they could not take away the last of the human freedoms: one's ability to choose his/her own attitude. Frankl realized that his ability to determine how he responded to his environment was psychological and that his human spirit was still free. With this in mind, he found daily existential meaning and purpose in aiding other prisoners by sharing the little food he did have and offering comforting words.

Unlike our man in the boxcar who went down the path of negativity, Frankl chose a path of positive empowerment. Both men had response-ability. If Frankl could find meaning in and survive the horrific experience of the concentration camps, and a man can freeze to death in a non-freezing boxcar, imagine what your response-ability can do for you. Imagine what you can endure. Have you see the movie *The Lone Survivor*? That movie shows what the human will can endure. Can you survive the perceived challenges of your everyday life and maintain a positive attitude? Absolutely! To be a peak performer, a sense of response-ability is a must.

EVENT + RESPONSE = OUTCOME

There is a simple math equation that I want you to learn and, more importantly, implement on a daily basis.

E [Event] + R [Response] = O [Outcome]

In life, it is not what happens to you; it is how you handle what happens to you. It is your ability to respond (response-ability) that is going to determine your outcome when adversity is thrown your way.

As a human being, YOU have the ability to respond to an event in the manner you deem appropriate. The response is your choice. Humans have the unique ability to socialize their innate responses to events with the three steps of performance improvement: (1) awareness, (2) strategy and (3) implementation of the strategy. We have previously discussed this process, and it provides an essential foundation for full comprehension of E + R = O.

We often do not have much control over the Events in our lives, but we do control our Responses. This is an empowering notion, because once you realize that you control half the equation, you recognize that you control half the outcome. If a negative event occurs and you keep a positive present-moment focus with a big-picture mentality and a "Compared to what?" perspective as your response, then you will significantly influence the outcome in your favor.

This is the process of mental conditioning that you prepare for thoroughly establishing mental routines. The practice of mental conditioning will teach you how to be responsible by accepting the Events, formulating Responses and, therefore, perceiving the Outcomes.

We are all capable of using this process to our benefit in life because we all have the ability to control our responses. We all have personal power.

THE HUMAN PAUSE

As was briefly mentioned, humans have the unique ability to become internally aware of their responses to external stimuli. The famous psychological study known as Pavlov's Dog Experiments represents groundbreaking research investigating conditioned and unconditioned responses to unconditioned and conditioned stimuli. Without going into all the details of classical (Pavlovian) conditioning, the takeaway relevant to mental conditioning is when there is a stimulus, there is a response.

Humans are no different, except for our ability to become aware of our responses. This recognition of how we respond is vital to mental conditioning, because we can train ourselves to pause in between the stimulus and our response, again giving us personal power to choose our response. Once we are aware of our innate responses to certain stimuli, we have the power to control and change them. Most people are unaware of this unique human ability, and these are the people we say have poor self-control skills. What they have is a non-trained pause to adversity and negative events.

Start becoming aware of how you respond to certain stimuli. To gain awareness and challenge yourself to catch that pause in between the event and your reaction, reflect on how you react to particular events. Those trained in discipline and response-ability face adverse stimuli with poise. They control their pause by taking a deep breath and responding in a manner conducive to the attainment of excellence. Developing control over that pause is what separates those who stay in control under pressure and those who crack.

Remember it this way: When the dog of adversity threatens with his dangerous jaws, control yourself with your human pause… and deep breath.

EMOTION CLOUDS REALITY

In the heat of competition, it is easy for your mind to become clouded by adversity. When officials make poor calls, the opposition seems to be catching lucky breaks, or you are just not performing to your full potential on that day, it is easy to let your emotions get the best of your performance. As a football player in pursuit of excellence, do not let your emotions cloud the reality of performance.

When you take emotion out of the picture, you tend to respond much more clearly. What does emotion do? Emotion clouds reality. In my work in the mental game of football, I see frustrated people fire off at officials, coaches, players and athletic directors. These people often approach minor and trivial situations as if they were life or death, not football. Most times after the outburst, there's regret that emotions overpowered sensible response-ability.

It is important to use the mental conditioning skills we've discussed in this manual to maintain response-ability. This comes back to self-control – recognizing what is within your control and emotionally letting go of everything else. Rely on the "3P's" of peak performance (present, process, positive) as the conscience that reminds you of your ability to respond with excellence rather than emotion. Act out of routine and conditioned/trained response, not emotion.

RAVIZZA'S RULES OF CONTROL

The greatest coach I have ever had was my mentor at Cal State Fullerton, and he is an icon in the field of sport psychology. Dr. Ken Ravizza introduced me to his three rules of mental conditioning that I believe truly reflect the significance of response-ability as it relates to football.

I believe a peak performer on the gridiron must understand those rules of response-ability to give himself the personal power to reach the summit of The Mountain of Excellence:

1. Before you can control your performance, you must be in control of yourself.

2. You have very little control of what goes on around you, but you have total control over how you choose to respond to it.

3. What you are aware of you can control; what you are unaware of will control you.

Staying in control of yourself and recognizing what you can and cannot control will allow you to mentally stay in a calm, centered and grounded place. Staying in control of yourself in the face of adversity is a skill set that must be repetitively practiced for its proper development and will allow you to perform in pressure situations.

Understanding what you can and cannot control, and choosing to focus on what you can control while letting go of what you cannot, gives you the personal power to focus your time, energy and attention to achieve excellence.

The first step to self-control is having an awareness of what is going on around you and, more importantly, what is going on inside of you. Ultimately, the development of self-awareness will place the power of response-ability in your head and in your hands.

CAIN'S COACHING POINT:
Early on in the manual, you learned the importance of forcing yourself to act differently than how you feel, shouldering that personal response-ability, and choosing to act appropriately regardless of the situation. How have you been doing **at acting differently than how you feel? Where in your life can you act differently than how you feel, choosing your response, and giving yourself a better chance for success?**

_____

_____

_____

PRAYER, PRIMAL, PERFECT?

In his book *Heads-Up Baseball*, Dr. Ken Ravizza points out that when athletes get emotionally out of control, it usually manifests through their performance in three general ways. They become a Prayer, Primal, or Perfect performer, all of which lead to a decreased level of performance.

PRAYER: When you become the prayer player, you look to some higher power to help you perform. You resign to faith in fate and simply hope for the stars to align and present you with the desired result.

PRIMAL: When you become a primal player, you resort back to the days of the caveman. You begin to perform in a desperate and erratic manner that often leaves you out of control and emotionally frustrated, and the desired result remains elusive.

PERFECT: When you become the perfect player, you attempt to make everything perfect. You strive for performance perfection and little mistakes prevent you from appreciating the beautiful imperfections of the game. As we have discussed, performance oriented around perfection is a sure path to failure because nothing is perfect. Remember, performance is not about perfection; it is about progress.

As a performer, you DO NOT want to fall under any of these three categories of Prayer, Primal or Perfect.

The defining question at the highest levels of competition is not who has the most physical talent, because physical talent is, for the most part, similar at the highest levels of performance. Were the Seahawks 40pts more talented than the Denver Broncos at Super Bowl XLVIII? Instead, the question pertains to who is able to bring his mental talents to the table on a consistent basis and who has the ability to respond appropriately under the pressures of adversity.

As a football player, you want to move away from Prayer, Primal and Perfect and into PREPARED and PRESENT. Mental preparation will assist you in the development of appropriate response-ability, giving yourself the best opportunity for performance excellence, one play at a time.

TRAIN YOUR RESPONSE-ABILITY

Coach Bear Bryant understood that football was the premiere vehicle for training response-ability. When he arrived at Alabama in 1958, he said: "We are going to do two things. We are going to learn to play football, and we are going to get up and go to class like our mamas and papas expect us to. And we are going to win. Ten years from now, you are going to be married with a family. Your wife might be sick, your kids might be sick, you might be sick, but you will get your butt up and go to work. That's what I'm going to do for you. I'm going to teach you how to do things you don't feel like doing."

Peak performance is contingent on personal response-ability in daily excellence. Excellence is largely about being accountable for your perspective and controlling your response to the adverse events that will inevitably occur during performance. Use the equation $E + R = O$ as a reminder that you control half of the equation and the outcome is a result of your perspective. When you train your response-ability, you place the power in your head.

All peak performers learn to take ownership of their past, command the present, and take charge of their future. Once you instill these values within your performance, you will gain the self-control necessary for performance excellence. Do not become a victim to events. Become a champion by developing the ability to respond appropriately to adversity. We all have the ability to respond appropriately, and the material throughout this book gives you the resources to do just that.

The Mountain of Excellence and the game of football call out to many performers, but the ones who reach the peak are those who have the response-ability to master the journey and overcome the adversity. The Mountain of Excellence will put obstacles in your path and will humble you at times, just like football and just like life.

CHAPTER #8 REVIEW

☐ If it is to be, it is up to me.

☐ Response-ability is taking ownership of your past, commanding your present and taking charge of your future.

☐ Event + Response = Outcome.

☐ When the dog of adversity threatens with his dangerous jaws, control yourself with your human pause.

☐ Emotion clouds reality; learn to control it.

☐ Develop self-control by learning the three rules of response-ability.

☐ Prayer, Primal and Perfect are all undesirable states of performance mentality.

CHAPTER #9

RELAX & RECOVER
MENTAL IMAGERY

> "Coaches get Wednesday, Thursday, Friday and a walk-through on Saturday. That's our time to help you guys get ready to play. Sunday's your day. We're going to make some adjustments, as you know, but we're not going to be telling you where to line up and where to go and what to do. That's your day to relax and perform."
>
> **Jon Gruden**
> **Former NFL Head Coach**

Most football coaches and players I work with have a hard time relaxing. This is often due to the combative nature and the aggressive mentality it takes to play this physical game at a high level. As a peak performer, you spend a lot of time acting differently than how you feel and forcing yourself to keep on grinding and working to take your performance to the next level.

Another reason why many football coaches and players have a hard time relaxing is that a large part of their lives is spent making themselves do the things they may not feel like doing but that are instrumental to peak performance on the gridiron. This shows their necessary dedication and resolve to being the best; however, quality time devoted to relaxation and recovery is also necessary to maximize performance potential. *The harder you work, the more important recovery is to regeneration so that you can continue to work and train at a high level.*

The ability to relax is essential to peak performers, and it is fundamental to developing peace of mind both during and away from the field. When it comes to your ability to relax, you cannot make yourself relax; you must *let* yourself relax, and this is where football players and coaches often find the challenge.

This performance state seems diametrically opposed to the intense focus demanded for performance excellence on the field and is therefore difficult for most to achieve. When you are in a relaxed state, however, your heart rate is lower, your breathing becomes deeper, and this kick-starts the recovery/repair process for the body and brain. The more relaxed you are, the quicker you recover from the demands you place on yourself and the quicker you can get back to performance and preparation at the highest level.

CAIN'S COACHING POINT:
Relaxation is a skill that must be practiced and is a skill that can be developed with proper training, just like the fundamental physical skills of playing football.

THE ABILITY TO RELAX IS INSIDE YOU

Everything you need to relax is already inside you. The world's most powerful tranquilizers already reside within your body. You have the ability to use these tranquilizers to put yourself to sleep at night, and you can train yourself to tap into one of the most powerful resources of your body and mind throughout the day when you experience stress, pressure and anxiety.

Football players have reported to me that if they could relax, it would help their performance. Knowing they need to relax is not the problem; the problem is that they often do not know how, because they have never been taught the simple strategy for relaxation.

Let's face it. When a coach or teammate says to you, "Hey, Brian, just relax!" (which I heard my entire career as an athlete) it does nothing to help your performance. In reality, it often makes you more tense, because now you know that your teammate or coach has picked up on the fact that you are stressed out and full of anxiety. As a player or coach, instead of telling someone to relax, ask him to take a good deep breath. Taking a deep breath is the single most valuable and effective exercise the athlete must learn to use to enter a more relaxed and present state.

THE CALMING OF CAIN

When I was a college baseball player at The University of Vermont, and a high school quarterback, the part of my game that held me back the most was my inability to relax and keep my mind productively focused in the present moment, one pitch/play at a time. My mind would get moving so fast that I could not keep it on the one thought that mattered, the execution of that particular pitch/play. My mind would be thinking about how this was my opportunity to make up for my previous mistakes; to finally show my coaches, teammates, and myself that I was good; that I was worthy of the scholarship or the playing time I had been given; and that, if I could perform at the level of my expectations, I could be one of the best.

As you can tell, the gears would begin to move faster and faster until I could hardly breathe; and before I knew it, I was ready to come out of the game before it even started.

My senior year of college I took a stress management class with the University of Vermont gymnastics coach Gary Bruning. Luckily for me, it was more of an applied stress management class than a theory-based class. He taught the class **how** to mentally and physically relax instead of teaching textbook theories of stress management and all the physiological effects of stress that I had experienced. I was very aware of the fact I did not know how to relax, so I embraced the opportunity for self-improvement as Coach Bruning taught us all how to relax.

He had us lie down on the floor and talked us through a deep-breathing exercise. I put my hand on my stomach and focused intently on breathing in through my nostrils and out through my mouth, while feeling my stomach rise with the inhalation and lower with the exhalation of each breath. After about 5 minutes of feeling weird just lying there and feeling like I should be doing something else, with my mind racing 100MPH, I finally experienced my mind slowing down and my body and mind relaxing.

I was 22 years old, a senior in college, and I can still vividly remember experiencing the ability to relax for the first time in my life. It was a revolutionary mind-body experience, and utterly unfamiliar to me. I could slow my mind down and focus into the present through my newfound ability to relax. I could now also speed up my recovery process simply by focusing on my breathing. To this day, I am grateful that I enrolled in that course and for Coach Bruning's applied method of teaching.

MAXIMIZING OXYGEN IN THE OCTAGON

 As a mental conditioning coach, nowhere have I seen relaxation and deep breathing serve a more vital function for performance excellence than in the Ultimate Fighting Championship. The world's most combative, most competitive sport of mixed martial arts is a ballet of violence by nature. Some people may find it too brutal for their liking, but this cannot discredit the impressive mentality it takes to step inside of the Octagon and go to battle. As athletes and coaches, we can learn a lot from what happens mentally inside the Octagon that can assist peak performance in football. In my work with college and high school football programs, I teach a lot of the very same mental skills that I train the best MMA fighters on the planet to have in their mental game arsenal.

In mixed martial arts, it is often the fighter who can relax first and move the fight into his specialty who wins. While the fighters work on bringing the fight to them, some of the greatest coaches in the game can be heard reinforcing the importance of breathing to help their fighter athletes relax. As a coach, the verbal cue for an athlete to take a breath is a reminder of what the athlete must do to calm down and perform at a more relaxed state. The more an athlete practices his breathing exercises to relax and quiet his mind outside of the Octagon, the more the brain and body know how to respond when he takes the deep breath inside the Octagon. As with everything in peak performance, you must learn to be in control of yourself physically and mentally before you can control your performance, and the most crucial practice to gain self-control is deep breathing.

I see getting an MMA fighter to take a deep breath in his

corner between rounds the same as a football player taking a deep breath pre-snap and a coach getting his team to take good deep breaths at the start of a time-out.

RELAXED INTENSITY – CONTROLLED RAGE

The best football players perform with a relaxed intensity. These players become so immersed in their present-moment focus of execution on that one play that they are simultaneously calm and poised, yet fully engaged and energized. Their competitive concentration appears unbreakable. Nothing can distract them; no adversity fazes them. They are "locked in" and it is as if they are playing on another level. Well, they ARE on another level; this is performance excellence!

CAIN'S COACHING POINT:
This peak performance state of excellence is different than "The Zone." Personally, I believe "The Zone" to be a place of quiet mind and quiet body where you are performing at your best.

I think "The Zone" is a place that we waste too much time talking about and trying to get to. I do not believe you can recreate "The Zone," but I do believe that you can get much closer to the state of peak performance through mental conditioning of distraction control, battling and dealing with adversity, acting differently than you feel, and competing all out, every play. I invest my time in coaching how to mentally persevere and have good bad days; I do not focus on getting into "The Zone." Remember, you cannot always control how you feel, but you can choose how you act. Think of confidence as an ACTION more than a feeling.

RELAX FOR RESULTS

Many coaches will ask me to teach them the secret of performance when the pressure to produce results is at its highest. They want me to teach their team how to produce when it is late in the 4th quarter and the game is on the line. What they fail to understand, however, is that there is no secret key to unlock performance when you need it the most. The best way a player or team can respond to the situation is to relax and trust in his mental and physical conditioning. This gives him the best chance to execute on the next play - and executing on the next play is ALL THAT MATTERS!

So when coaches ask me this question, they are usually surprised when I lead the team away from their performance arena to a quiet and controlled environment and instruct them in methods of breathing and relaxation. The football player must be able to relax in a quiet and controlled environment before he will ever be able to relax in the face of adversity on the field. The deep breath and ability to relax is the most powerful tool in the peak performance toolbox and is critical to unlocking your potential so that you can become "locked in" during performance.

RELAXATION IS A SKILL ANYONE CAN DEVELOP

As with all mental conditioning techniques, relaxation is a skill that can be learned and developed through training. Relaxation is a skill that requires mastering all the material previously covered in this book. The ability to relax is founded upon a present-moment focus on the process of what you can control, along with a perspective of positivity that has been practiced over and over so that it has become routine.

I want you to think of the ability to relax as a skill just like the physical skills you use in football. If you can throw, kick or catch a football, your ability to execute that skill is because you have trained yourself to perform it. You have practiced and you have conditioned that skill, investing time and effort into improving it. I want you to do the same for the mental conditioning skill of relaxation.

THE 5-4-3-2-1 RELAXATION/FOCUS EXERCISE

I want to walk you through a relaxation and focus exercise called the 5-4-3-2-1 exercise. By understanding how to breathe properly and practicing the process of a 5-4-3-2-1 relaxation technique until it becomes a routine relaxation procedure, you give yourself the best opportunity to relax under pressure and perform at your best.

CAIN'S COACHING POINT:
I have created a 5-4-3-2-1 relaxation training audio that you can download for free by subscribing to my podcast at www.briancain.com/podcast. There are other great training tools available for you on my podcast as well.

TWO TYPES OF BREATHING

There are two types of breathing: diaphragmatic breathing and shoulder breathing. Diaphragmatic breathing is deep breathing, using your diaphragm and abdominal muscles. To identify this type of breathing, place your hand upon your stomach and feel your abdominal muscles expand as you inhale and contract as you exhale. During this deep breathing, air entirely fills your lungs and maximizes oxygen intake. Shoulder breathing, on the other hand, only reaches the top of your lungs. Often referred to as shallow breathing, shoulder breathing is often the result of a performer's inability to relax, resulting in tight muscles which exacerbate this tight breathing. As a performer, you must learn the proper method of deep breathing.

It is also important to know where to breathe. For proper relaxation, one should inhale through the nose, because the nose acts as a natural air filter, and exhale out your mouth, giving you a more forceful release. As you inhale, I want you to think about a count of 4-6; and then as you exhale, think about a count of 6-8, making your exhalation a little bit longer than your inhalation.

SCRIPT FOR THE 5-4-3-2-1 RELAXATION SESSION

This is a script that you can read to your team to help them practice and develop the skill of relaxation. You will want to read it slowly and in a monotone voice.

The first thing you want to do is put yourself in a quiet, comfortable environment. Sit up straight in your chair, hands in your lap or on the desk in front of you, feet flat on the floor. Please look at a spot on the wall in front of you, and focus on that spot.

Now, let your eyes gently close as you inhale, breathing deeply through your nose. As you inhale, your shoulders and chest should not move. Focus on breathing steadily and deeply through the nose, pushing out all your abdominal muscles as your diaphragm expands and air fills the bottom of your lungs. Now, exhale through your mouth, as your abdominal muscles and diaphragm contract and the air exits your lungs.

As you continue to focus on your breathing, having a count of 4-6 on the inhalation and 6-8 on the exhalation, realize that everything you need to relax is already inside you. The world's most powerful tranquilizers lay within. The ability to relax is a skill that needs to be developed and you are doing that now. You need to train to relax just like you do for the skills required to play football.

Answer the following three questions as you continue to focus on your breathing. Answer these questions in your mind and notice how the answers just pop into your head:

1. What is 3 x 3?

2. What is your middle name?

3. What street did you grow up on?

Notice how easily and effortlessly the answers popped into your mind. The ability to relax is a skill that can be trained, developed and called upon just as easily as answering those three questions.

We will now go through a short body scan in which you are to focus your awareness into the body parts that are mentioned.

When you hear the number 5, let your toes, the balls of your feet, arches, heels, your ankles, your Achilles tendon, your calves and your shins release, relax and let go.

When you hear the number 4, let your knees, your quads, your hamstrings, your gluteus maximus, your groin, your hips, your whole lower body release, relax and let go, sinking further and further into the chair that you are sitting on.

When you hear the number 3, let your lower back, your mid back, your upper back, your abs, your obliques, your ribs, your pectorals, your whole torso release, relax and let go.

What you will find is that the more relaxed you become, the better you might feel; and the better you feel, the more relaxed you will want to become.

When you hear the number 2, relax your traps, your shoulders, your biceps, your triceps, your forearms, your hands, your fingers - just release, relax and let go.

When you hear the number 1, relax the back of your neck, the back of your head, the top of your head, your forehead, your eyes, your cheeks, your jaw; let your lips gently part and your tongue hang in your mouth as a complete and total body of relaxation takes over.

What you will realize is that the more relaxed you become, the better you will feel; and the better you feel, the more relaxed you will want to become.
Take another deep breath.

Now, gently open your eyes and bring yourself back to this moment, right here, right now.

This concludes the 5-4-3-2-1 relaxation session.

CONTROL THE ENVIRONMENT

In order to properly condition your relaxation, you must begin training in a controlled environment. Initial relaxation training should occur in a quiet and controlled environment where you can relax in peace. This enables you to focus on the process of relaxation in that moment, ignoring all other stimuli and emptying the mind of unnecessary thoughts.

After you have practiced in this controlled and quiet environment for a few weeks, slowly integrate adversity to simulate a more chaotic or competitive environment similar to a football game.

Introduce crowd noise or music in the background of your controlled setting and practice your relaxation response to this adversity by focusing on your breathing. Audio simulates adversities that will become distractions if you let them get into your head. Do not let them get in your head; instead, focus on the next breath. Use your relaxed state of mind to push distractions far away by locking into what you want to focus on, going one breath at a time.

Once you have trained your ability to relax under simulated adversity in a controlled environment, the next step is to perform your relaxation technique in performance practices, and then pressure-packed scenarios in game-like practices. During these preparation sessions, you will further practice the execution of your relaxation techniques, and eventually this will translate to an execution and peak performance during games.

CONTROL YOURSELF

As I am sure you have gathered by now, breathing is the foundation for relaxation. Simultaneously, breathing is the basis for emotional state management, aka self-control. Relaxation conditions self-control by teaching you how to become grounded within the self. Your body and mind become one in the present moment as you focus on the breathing. The relaxation process is proven to reduce stress levels and alleviate anxiety, giving you control of your emotional state. Good breathing makes all the difference in self-control, and thus in the achievement of performance excellence.

CONDITIONING THE RELAXATION RESPONSE

If you have never trained your breathing and you try to relax by taking a deep breath in a pressure situation, the body and the brain will not be conditioned to respond by gaining control of yourself. If you condition yourself to relax through the routine practice of deep breathing, first in the quiet, controlled environment and then in more disruptive scenarios, by the time you call upon it in the heat of competition on the gridiron, it will be a skill you have developed and it will be there when you need it.

When you practice the 5-4-3-2-1 technique, you will feel more connected to the present moment, more relaxed and more in control of yourself. The more you train with the 5-4-3-2-1 technique, the more you focus on your breathing and the more you do your relaxation training, the more this relaxation preparation is going to help in practices and games. The goal is for this technique to become so routine that when you take a deep breath to help you relax, your body will be conditioned to respond by relaxing and getting you in a place of self-control. When this occurs, you will know you have a properly conditioned relaxation response.

RELAXATION IN THE RECOVERY PROCESS

For football players to take their performance to the next level, they must constantly put their bodies and minds in uncomfortable and stressful situations where they are challenged to adapt and evolve. To consistently bring a high level of energy and effort to these situations, players must be able to recover outside of the competitive arena.

Relaxation is a tremendous facilitator of recovery. The more relaxed you are, the greater the recovery process, thus assisting your physical and mental regeneration so that you can continue to compete and train at your highest level.

> "You can't be a party animal and a champion."
>
> *John Aloisi*
> *Head Football Coach*
> *Shrewsbury HS, Shrewsbury, Massachusetts*

RECOVERY PROCESS

As you are probably well aware, there is a physical recovery process after physical performance in which the body goes to work repairing the damage done to muscle tissue. After a weight lifting session, it is this physical recovery process that builds the muscle you desire for performance. Not surprisingly, there is a mental recovery process of releasing performance stress and anxiety that is equally important. In the process, these two forms of recovery often converge, blending similar practices and exercises to maximize both forms of recovery. All athletes should be aware of the significance of recovery on performance and understand that both your physical and mental recoveries are enhanced when in a relaxed state.

CAIN'S CHALK TALK:
If you were to grade your ability to relax on a 1-10 scale, with 10 being the best, you would give yourself a grade of ?

1 2 3 4 5 6 7 8 9 10

To help me move one number closer to 10, I will do the following:

_____

_____

THE MAGIC 20-MINUTE WINDOW OF RECOVERY

Dr. Declan Connolly is a world-renowned exercise physiologist, sports nutritionist, and strength and conditioning coach. He is a professor at The University of Vermont and a consultant to the New York Rangers, among other professional teams and Olympic organizations. He also was my college undergraduate advisor at The University of Vermont and remains to this day a close personal friend and mentor on the physiological aspects of performance. Dr. Connolly speaks of the importance of the sports nutrition magic 20-minute window.

The magic 20-minute window of sports nutrition indicates that you want to have food in your system, whether it is a protein shake, a peanut butter and jelly sandwich or even a Snickers bar, within the 20-minute period after finishing a workout to help speed up the recovery process.

The recovery benefits of getting food in your system within 20 minutes after the completion of a workout will be greater than if you had steak and potatoes 45 minutes to 1 hour after a workout. Physically and mentally, the recovery process is kick-started when you can get these much-needed proteins, carbohydrates, and fats into your system within that window. Developing the discipline to bring food with you for post-performance snacks is important to enhance your recovery process. It is equally important that you force yourself to act on your knowledge of recovery, because many athletes report they do not feel like eating after performance. If you let your feelings dictate your actions, you lose in football and in life.

DISCIPLINE IS THE KEY TO RECOVERY

The hardest part about eating inside of the magic 20-minute window after completing a workout is having the discipline to bring food with you to the gym or the field. Establishing a disciplined routine of bringing yourself a simple peanut butter and jelly sandwich on wheat bread, or a piece of fruit, and getting that food in your system within that 20-minute window will dramatically speed up your recovery process.

ONE-THIRD OF YOUR LIFE – INVEST IN A BED

If you knew you were going to spend one-third of your life performing a sport, you would want to gather all the information you could and educate yourself on how to achieve performance excellence in that sport. If you knew you were going to work a specific job for one-third of your life, I bet you would also want to become as knowledgeable and proficient as possible to achieve job performance excellence. So why would sleep, which you will do for approximately one-third of your life, be any different? Unfortunately, you probably know very little about what goes on physiologically when you sleep, so let's get you started with some general knowledge about the importance of sleep for your recovery. It is the #1 most important factor and place that you can get a competitive advantage.

POWER SLEEP

Dr. James Maas is a professor at Cornell University and one of the world's leading authorities and experts on sleep. In his book *Power Sleep*, he breaks down the information you need to know about sleeping and how much you need it to perform at your peak. As a scholar, he has addressed the physiological benefits of sleep and the issue of severe sleep deprivation that plagues most college and high school athletes, resulting in performances that represent about 80% of their potential.

An individual is considered to be sleep deprived if they sleep four hours or less per night, while eight hours constitutes normal sleep. The National Sleep Foundation's sleep guidelines recommend seven to nine hours for the average adult. Dr. Maas suggests in *Power Sleep* that you get 9 hours and 15 minutes of sleep a night so that you will receive your five REM (Rapid Eye Movement) cycles, thus maximizing the physiologic benefits of your recovery time in sleep. One night of missed sleep will probably do little harm, but the cumulative effect of poor sleep will have a negative impact on your performance.

Sleep is an active physiological process, one in which your body is busy carrying out vital activities while you are unconscious. While asleep, your body alternates between two forms of sleep: rapid eye movement (REM) and non-REM sleep. This cycle repeats several times throughout the night. The stage of REM sleep provides the brain with the energy to support it during waking hours and is necessary for restoring the mind to function at a level of peak performance. These physiological processes are significant for your psyche, because mental conditioning is most effective when an individual's psychological state is in sync with an optimum physiological state.

10 TIPS FOR SOUND SLEEPING

1. **Relax Before Retiring** – Take some time for a pre-sleep ritual to break the connection between stress and bedtime. Try listening to the 5-4-3-2-1 relaxation session, listen to relaxation music, do some light stretching or take a hot shower.

2. **Watch the Caffeine** – Caffeine is the stimulant present in coffee (100-200 mg), soda (50-75 mg), tea (50-75 mg), and various over-the-counter medications. Caffeine should not be consumed for at least four to six hours before bedtime.

3. **Watch the Alcohol** – Although alcohol is a depressant and may

help you fall asleep, the subsequent metabolism that clears it from your body when you are sleeping causes a withdrawal syndrome. This withdrawal causes awakenings and is often associated with nightmares and sweats. To help reduce some of these effects, try drinking one glass of water for every alcoholic beverage consumed. You should stop all liquid consumption at least two hours before bedtime so that you are not waking up in the middle of the night to urinate.

4. **Exercise at the Right Time** – Regular exercise relieves stress and encourages good sleep. However, if a little exercise really gets your blood pumping, it would be wise to avoid working out in the evening or just before bedtime.

5. **Cut Down on Noise, Light, and Extreme Temperatures** – Try earplugs, a night-light, an eye mask or drape clip. The best temperature for sleep is 65-69 degrees.

6. **Eat Right and Sleep Tight** – Avoid eating a large meal just before bedtime or going to bed hungry. It is about balance. Also, whenever possible, opt for foods that promote sleep, such as milk, tuna, halibut, artichokes, oats, asparagus, potatoes and bananas.

7. **Understanding Jet Lag** – Before you cross time zones, try waking up later or earlier to help your body adjust to the time difference. It takes approximately one day for each hour you fly to adjust to a new time zone. Many people are affected more severely by West to East travel than East to West. Anticipate that it may take a few days for your body to catch up, and you can speed up that process by easing yourself on the new time zone schedule before you leave.

8. **Respect the Purpose of the Bed** – Avoid TV, eating, and emotional discussions while in bed. The mind and body associate bedtime activities with being in bed. Do not let a bad habit keep you awake.

9. **Nap Smart** – A power nap early in the afternoon can really refresh you. Make it brief - no more than 20 minutes. Sleep too much and you may spend the night staring at the ceiling.

10. **Pet Sleepers** - Does your pet sleep with you? This, too, may cause arousals from either allergies or their movements in the bed. Thus, Fido and Kitty may be better off on the floor than on your sheets.

Be sure to invest in the best mattress you can afford. How you spend the eight hours a night you invest in bed will determine how you are able to invest the other 2/3 of your life that day. Invest in yourself. Invest in your rest and recovery. Invest in the best mattress you can buy.

OLYMPIC SLEEP TRICKS

The USA Olympic organization will often go into the Olympic Village ahead of the games and put in extended-length beds and blackout curtains in the rooms of all its athletes. This is because the organization recognizes how important sleep is to its athletes' peak performance. The USOC wants to give our athletes the best opportunity to bring home the gold and so it invests wisely in sleep.

You probably cannot travel with blackout curtains, but you can get a pair of earplugs and an eye mask for under $10.00. If you are a high school or college student and you are living in a dorm where people come home late at night slamming doors, roommates make noise and there is a constant commotion, make the investment in your sleep time by getting earplugs that will block much of that noise and an eye mask to shut out the excess light. Both items will help with your ability to get an excellent night's sleep. You may also want to try one of the many sleep noise apps on your phone.

CAIN'S EXPENSIVE EXPERIENCE ON RECOVERY

When I was an athlete, I always thought I was capable of more than was requested of me and that the longer and harder I worked, the better I would become. I was constantly working out and running, doing more than was expected. What I failed to realize was the significant difference between working harder versus working smarter, and that the more I worked, the more I needed to recover.

I never had a plan for recovery or for a great sleep routine, and I probably slept around 4-6 hours a night in college. As a result, I broke down physically and mentally, and I was injured all the time. I was the guy who pulled all-nighters, thinking I could cram all my studying into one or two days and then regurgitate it on exam day. I would either take course exams so jacked up on caffeine that I would crash in the middle of it, or I would walk in and simply not recall any of the information because I was so tired. If you are a casualty of poor recovery habits, *Power Sleep* can help you with its review of the physiological and psychological problems that come with pulling all-nighters.

YOGA AS A MENTAL CONDITIONING EXERCISE

Again, it was my course with Coach Bruning that turned my life and recovery routines in a productive and progressive direction. In this course, Coach Bruning taught yoga to the class as a source of both physiological and psychological relaxation. Practicing and understanding the benefits of yoga have really helped me become more familiar with my body and in managing my emotional state. During that course, I improved my flexibility and learned how to breathe and find my center of balance, both physically and mentally. Ironically, before the 2013-2014 NFL season there was a fantastic article on ESPN.com about the Seattle Seahawks and how they used yoga as a part of their pre-practice routine to gain better control of their breath and their physical/mental/ emotional self.

RE-CENTER YOURSELF

Relaxation and recovery are both critical elements within a peak performer's mental conditioning program. Training your relaxation response through deep breathing will help you stay locked into the present moment, think more clearly, and perform more fluidly during competition. Relaxation outside of the competitive arena will help you speed up the recovery process, enabling you to return and perform harder, longer and smarter as you take your football performance to the next level.

Throughout life, it is important to use these relaxation and recovery practices to constantly re-center yourself, because internal balance leads to the performance consistency necessary for all peak performers. As you climb The Mountain of Excellence, remember to pause, take a deep breath and re-center yourself This will keep you climbing at your most productive pace and playing football one play at a time.

MENTAL IMAGERY

At this moment, imagine standing on a stage that is situated in an enormous stadium. As you look around, you suddenly realize the air is being filled by thunderous applause reverberating around the arena. The stadium is full of people and they are standing up out of their seats. As you remain on the stage, taking in the sights and the sounds, you realize this standing ovation is for you.

It is a trophy ceremony at the championship parade and you are the MVP! You turn to your right and left and high five and hug your jubilant teammates. You seek out your coach for more celebration and then you look out into the stands for your family. It is a moment like no other!

A voice over the loudspeaker announces the beginning of the trophy presentation. The trophy is handed over to the head coach, who passes it to his assistants, and then it makes its way to the players.

As you get your hands on the trophy, you raise it above your head, the crowd responds with another great wave of applause, and you return the acknowledgement with a smile. As you stand there with the physical manifestation of the title, a final and total comprehension of your achievement washes over you. This is it. In this moment, you have reached the mountaintop.

There on the stage, you stand at the pinnacle of football at your level. You stand a champion. With utmost satisfaction, you know you have given your best when you needed it the most and that your performance has been simply superior to the competition. Your PRIDE - that Personal Responsibility In Daily Excellence, your making all of your todays count and not counting them over all those years of training - has culminated in this. The game has rewarded that PRIDE. Now, all the world watches and recognizes you as the ultimate peak performer, the epitome of performance excellence when it comes to football.

This imaginary scenario is your introduction to mental imagery.

Now, let's make that vision a reality.

CAIN'S COACHING POINT:
Everything happens twice. First in your mind, then in reality. Mental Imagery is one of the most well- researched mental skills that is NOT being used in football on a consistent basis. That means Mental Imagery is a place where you can get a competitive advantage and take your game to the next level.

HEAD REHEARSAL

One of the most underutilized mental conditioning skills in all of football is mental imagery. Mental imagery, often referred to as visualization, is the process of creating mental experiences that resemble actual physical experiences. Similar to watching a highlight video of your best performance in your mind.

This process is similar to the stimulation of the imagination when you read an excerpt in the second-person narrative, such as the introduction to this chapter. The difference is that the script is not on a piece of paper in front of you; it is all in your head.

In mental conditioning, mental imagery is used to enhance performance preparation and build confidence. It is a technique employed to exercise the mind by mentally creating the environment of performance competition and mentally performing the competitive tasks required in football in your mind. Mentally, you rehearse how you want to feel and how you want to perform, imagining the integration of your physical conditioning and your mental conditioning within your mind to see your best performance before you step out on the field of battle.

THE MIND-BODY CONNECTION

Mental imagery has the potential to make a HUGE impact in your football performance. Whether you vividly imagine or you physically execute your performance, the brain processes those two experiences with similar psychoneuromuscular pathways. Made simple, that means you are hardwiring your brain and body for peak performance.

Mental imagery is physiologically creating neural patterns in your brain in the same manner as the performance of a physical action. Essentially, if you are lying in bed at night and you practice mental imagery, you are imprinting the blueprint of your performance in your mind, further embedding those pathways and enhancing your capacity to achieve what it is you see in your mind when you step onto the field.

CAIN'S COACHING POINT:
Before you get carried away, however, let's get one thing clear: Mental imagery is not a substitute for physical preparation. This is not some shortcut or fast track to peak performance. Putting in the physical time is necessary. The mental conditioning technique of mental imagery enhances your physical abilities by deepening those psychoneuromuscular pathways in your brain. Mental imagery is utilized to maximize the efficiency and effectiveness of your physical preparation.

YOU ARE "THE ARCHITECT" OF YOUR VISION

In order to emphasize how an individual practices mental imagery, I've drawn a parallel to it and a concept from the Warner Brothers blockbuster movie *Inception.* In the film, a complex plot revolves around dreams and characters' movements in and out of the dream world. There are particular characters in the movie called "architects," who build infinitely detailed dream worlds that mirror reality. This movie is one of the ultimate mind-benders in cinema, and if you haven't seen it, I apologize for using this particular analogy. However, this concept of "architects" is exactly what you want to emulate in your process of mental imagery.

When you perform the mental conditioning technique of mental imagery, you create a mental world. You construct in your mind a psychological replica of your sport's competitive arena (locker room, football field, stadium, etc.), placing you and your opponent within that arena and lining up at the line of scrimmage. When you perform mental imagery, you want to build in the sense of sight, the sense of sound, and the sense of touch. You want to mentally experience the appearance of where you will be playing, the field, the uniforms of your opponent.

You want to experience the energy in the stadium. If you are playing away from home, imagine the away crowd heckling you from the sidelines. You want to experience yourself making the plays that will make the difference at game's end. Some athletes even integrate the familiar smells of their venue or the locker room into their mental imagery. The more details you construct as the architect of the video in your mind, the greater you enhance the effectiveness of the mental imagery experience.

PHYSIOLOGICAL BENEFITS FROM PSYCHOLOGICAL STIMULUS

If you are still a little skeptical about mental imagery, then I want to give you a little taste of the mind-body connection. I want you to experience the physiological response to the psychological stimulus of mental imagery. Before telling you to just go off and practice mental imagery, I will walk you through a scenario.

Whenever you perform mental imagery, recall and practice the techniques of relaxation to help you focus more clearly on the mental imagery process.

So sit back and focus on your breathing. Go through the process of relaxation and practice your deep breathing as you read the passage below, or have someone read it to you.

I am going to walk you through a scenario where you go into your kitchen, reach into your refrigerator, pull out a lemon, cut lemon wedges, and take a bite out of one of those lemon wedges. Read slowly and imagine the scenario in all its detail. Practice utilizing all your senses in this passage, because you want to make this scenario feel as real as possible in your mind.

THE LEMON EXPERIMENT

Start by taking 3 good breaths on a 4-6 count on your inhalation and on a 6-8 count on exhalation. Breathe in nice and deep through your nose and release out through your mouth.

Now, imagine walking into your kitchen at home. Feel what the floor feels like on your bare feet.

You are now standing in front of your refrigerator. See the refrigerator in front of you in all its detail. Now, extend your hand outward, reaching for the refrigerator door, and clasp its door handle.

As you open that refrigerator door, notice a nice big, bright yellow lemon on the top shelf.

Reach for it and grab it. As you hold it in the palm of your hand, see the skin and feel the coolness and texture of that lemon as you feel its weight in your hand.

Put that lemon on the counter, take a knife lying there, and use it to cut the lemon in half the long way. See the juice and the body of that lemon as the knife slices through. Smell the slightly sour scent released into the air. Take half of the cut lemon and cut it again, so that you have two equal wedges. See and feel the sting of the lemon juice on your wet fingertips. Breathe in that lemon scent swelling in the air.

Now gently place your fingers, wet with lemon juice, on either side of a lemon wedge and lift it off the counter. Bring it up to your mouth and close your lips around the wedge before sinking your teeth along the lemon rind and squeezing the lemon juice into your mouth. Feel the lemon juice squirt onto the back of your tongue and the back of your mouth. Feel that sensation at the back of your teeth as you press your tongue against them to get all the lemon juice.

Remove the lemon and place the deflated wedge back on the counter.

A TASTE OF THE IMAGE

Did you have a bit of a puckering sensation? Did your mouth salivate at the thought of the lemon taste? Could you smell that lemon or feel the sour juice sting your taste buds? Just thinking about the process of eating lemon made me salivate while I wrote this passage.

If you did receive any of those sensations as you read the passage, then you have now consciously experienced a physiological response (the body responding) to a psychological stimulus. This is a simple firsthand experience that emphasizes the shared psychoneuromuscular pathways of the brain and body. Remember this experience and try to simulate the realness of eating the lemon in your mental imagery when you visualize yourself playing your best football.

If you did not experience a physiological response, then you probably read the passage too fast and didn't immerse yourself in this psychological scenario... or maybe you just did not eat enough lemons as a kid! But seriously, in order to properly utilize mental imagery, you MUST use the techniques of relaxation that you have learned. You must become absolutely immersed in the present mental rehearsal you are performing, releasing all mental bricks and deflecting all distractions.

MENTAL REHABILITATION & MENTAL REPS

One of the best ways to maintain your edge while recovering from an injury is to use mental imagery to take mental reps. If you cannot practice football, there is no reason why you cannot mentally prepare yourself for physical performance. Often called mental reps, players use mental imagery to imagine themselves doing all of the physical skills they would be doing that day in practice - lining up behind offense as they run a play, getting a clear picture in your mind of what that play will look like before it is run, and then checking to see if you had the clear image of the right play. This mental rehabilitation really provides a huge psychological advantage in the physical rehabilitation process by keeping the performance-specific psychoneuromuscular pathways in your brain active and as sharp as possible.

When a player is finally physically ready to perform, those psychoneuromuscular pathways are as close to game-ready as they can possibly be. By maintaining active psychoneuromuscular pathways, there is no dusting off the mental cobwebs and there is no regaining your mental edge. Your brain has been mentally preparing during the whole process of rehab and is fit and ready for performance on the field. By knowing how to practice mental imagery, there is absolutely no reason to lose your mental edge and confidence of knowing the plays or what your alignment and assignment are for that play.

MENTAL IMAGERY PAYS BIG DIVIDENDS

When he first broke into the NFL in 2005, quarterback Matt Cassel was the backup for Tom Brady and the New England Patriots. In 2008, after a Week 1 season-ending injury to reigning NFL MVP Tom Brady, Cassel was thrust into the starting role on the Patriots' offense. These were big shoes to fill, but Cassel was surprisingly cool about the transition.

There was a great deal of fascination surrounding Cassel, due to his inexperience in the starting role. In fact, Cassel had not started as quarterback in a football game since he was in high school and, according to ESPN research, Cassel is the only known quarterback to start in the NFL without having been a starter in college. Cassel had attended the University of Southern California (USC) and had been the backup quarterback to Heisman trophy winners Carson Palmer (2002) and Matt Leinart (2004).

What made Cassel so quietly confident was his preparation, particularly his use of mental imagery. In a *Sports Illustrated* article, Cassel discussed how he would wear a helmet on the sideline with the Patriots and would hear the play being called in from the offensive coordinator. He would then call the play cadence out loud on the sideline, as if he were in the huddle.

When people asked him, "Why do you do that?" Cassel would respond: "I call that play out loud and then I visualize what the play would be. I then open my eyes, watch the field, and see if the image I had in my mind is what happens on the field. I play the game one play at a time mentally so that when I get thrown in the game as a backup quarterback, I am not surprised, I am not caught off guard, I am always right in the mix of that game mentally." **THIS IS WHAT A MENTAL REP IS ALL ABOUT!**

His mental imagery performance paid off as Cassel led the New England Patriots to an 11-5 season. Despite not making the postseason with their winning record, due to a highly competitive division, Cassel's season, based on his leadership and performance, was a success. At season's end, the Patriots used their franchise tag on him, extending him a one-year contract worth over $14 million, the largest one-year contract for an offensive player in NFL history. Cassel ended up leaving New England in an off-season trade to the Kansas City Chiefs, where he went on to sign a six-year, $62.7 million dollar contract. As you can see from the experience of Matt Cassel, mental imagery pays big dividends.

MENTAL PERFORMANCE BEFORE PHYSICAL PERFORMANCE

Tampa Bay Buccaneers cornerback Darrelle Revis is widely considered to be the best cornerback in the National Football League. What sets "Reeve" apart is that he matches his incredible physical skill set with a relentless work ethic and a dynamic approach to the mental game.

Revis explained his routine to author Nicholas Dawidoff in the book *Collision Low Crossers*. *"I follow the same routine since I've been a rookie. I'm very mental about the game. What I do when I watch film and when I look on the TV in my living room at home is I see the same thing over and over. To remember, I have to keep replaying it over and over in my head. I watch the receivers' body language and the routes. Then, when you're in the game, the crazy thing is you see it and the light comes on. Ding! Crazy! I just saw it all week, I can make a play on this one."*

VIDEO ENHANCEMENT

I cannot emphasize enough that when you are doing mental imagery, you want to make the experience as game-like as possible. You want to utilize all of your mental capacity to make the images appear vivid and clear. A technique sometimes used to assist mental imagery is watching video of yourself performing before you do mental imagery. Witnessing yourself play on tape is not only good for understanding how you perform, but also can aid the practice of mental imagery since using past performances to conjure images helps provide details to mentally rehearse future performances.

I encourage the athletes I work with to create a personal highlight video that they watch before they do mental imagery. This enables them to relive their best performances and then re-imagine their feelings in those scenarios through mental imagery.

PRACTICING ADVERSITY

A great way to utilize the benefits of mental imagery is to create a list of situations in your sport that make you uncomfortable and represent some form of adversity. Once you have made this list, use it as a checklist and use mental imagery to perform under each adverse scenario, executing exactly the way you want to in performance. This is similar to the favorite physical practice of children acting out a last-second scenario, where their team is down one and they complete the game-winning touchdown pass as time expires. Both practices deal with adverse situations and both imagine a desired outcome.

IMAGINE YOUR EXCELLENCE

Mental imagery is one of most basic and fundamental of all mental conditioning strategies; however, it is widely underused. Remember that actions speak louder than words. You now have a greater understanding of the power of mental imagery; you just need to DO mental imagery in order to increase your performance preparation and confidence.

4 STEPS OF MENTAL IMAGERY

Doing mental imagery is as easy as you closing your eyes and watching your human highlight reel in your mind. It does not need to get more complex than that. When I train coaches to take their teams through mental imagery the night before games, I outline four steps so that they have a rhythm and routine to follow.

1. **Relaxation** – Take them through the 5-4-3-2-1 technique.

2. **Confidence Conditioning** – Take them through the positive affirmations you want them to hear and that you want to embed into their mental game. Say each statement three times with enough time between statements so that the players can repeat them to themselves.

3. **Mental Recall** – Have the players recall and revisit their best football performances of all time. They replay those big hits and great plays in their minds as if the past were happening now.

4. **Mental Rehearsal** – Have the players go forward to their next performance and visualize how exactly they want to perform. You can talk them through very specific situations that you have been preparing for against your upcoming opponent.

MENTAL IMAGERY WHILE WATCHING FILM

Another great time to use mental imagery is while you are watching film. A great film-watching routine is to:

1. Show the name of the play that was run. If on defense, show how the offense lines up and tell the team what play they ran.

2. Players imagine executing exactly like they want to on that play.

3. Roll the play so you can see what actually happened.

4. Players grade themselves on their performance before any coach says anything so that the players have to take ownership and are more engaged in the film breakdown process.

5. Have players imagine executing the play exactly the way that they should have so they get the "corrective mental rep."

6. Then break down the play in as much detail as you can by asking questions of the players so they have to go inside of their own heads and search for the answer, making them more engaged in the learning process.

Following these six steps for each play should take around 1 minute per play if the coach has prepared the right way. Incorporating mental imagery into teaching through video is a great way to speed up the learning curve, and it dramatically enhances the effectiveness of your video sessions.

CHAPTER #9 REVIEW

☐ We all possess the ability to relax.

☐ Aim to perform with a relaxed intensity.

☐ Relaxation is the secret to results under pressure.

☐ Relaxation is a skill one must develop like any other physical skill.

☐ Diaphragmatic breathing is superior to shoulder breathing.

☐ Practice the 5-4-3-2-1 technique to build a relaxation response.

☐ Begin training your relaxation response in a controlled environment and progress under simulated adversity.

☐ Emotional state management is all about self-control and breathing.

☐ Relaxation is instrumental to recovery process.

☐ Invest in your sleep.

☐ Relaxation before bed facilitates productive sleep, benefiting physiological and psychological recovery.

☐ Mental conditioning is most effective when an individual's psychological state is reflective of an optimum physiological state.

☐ Internal balance leads to the performance consistency necessary for all peak performers.

☐ You cannot make yourself relax; you must *let* yourself relax.

☐ Mental imagery is the process of creating mental experiences that resemble physical experience.

☐ Mental performance physiologically creates neural patterns in your brain in the same manner as the performance of physical action.

☐ As a mental architect, you want to build experiences of all the senses within your mental performance.

☐ Mental imagery enhances psychoneuromuscular pathways to assist physical rehabilitation.

☐ Practice mental performance before beginning physical competition.

☐ Watching videos of your best performances benefits your mental imagery by giving you a positive visual.

☐ Practice handling adversity in mental imagery as you do during preparation.

CHAPTER #10

INSPIRATION & MOTIVATION

> "Building a motivated football team is easy. You simply eliminate those individuals who are not motivated."
>
> **JB Wells**
> **Head Football Coach**
> **Endicott College**

I was in Dallas, Texas, at a fair and on a stage was a big, muscular strongman performing some amazing feats of strength. He was ripping phone books in half and bending crowbars with his hands to the thunderous applause of his audience.

In one of his acts, he pulled out a lemon and squeezed all the juice out of that lemon and said: "Ladies and gentlemen, I am a strongman. I've squeezed all the juice out of this lemon. I will give $1,000 to anyone who can come up and extract one more drop."

In response, two giant Dallas Cowboy-like guys went on stage to give it a try. The first guy grabbed the lemon and gave it a good, hard squeeze. No drop! The crowd laughed in amusement as he stepped back to let his friend give the lemon a squeeze. The crowd went silent and watched the second guy give the lemon a squeeze, contorting his face in grimaced concentration. He suddenly released his grip with a gasp for air, but still not one drop of lemon juice.

The crowd laughed and applauded as the two men exited the stage. The strongman was left on stage holding his arms in the air with the lemon in his hand when he saw an old lady, who looked to be in her seventies, walking up the stairs onto the stage.

The strongman said: "Ma'am, for the sake of time, can we move on? You are not going to squeeze any juice out of the lemon. I mean, c'mon. The guys who just tried couldn't do it and they looked like professional football players."

"Sir, just give me a chance," the old lady said politely.

"Okay. Here you go. One chance," said the strongman, who handed her the lemon as the crowd cheered in support.

The old lady took the lemon within her hands and began to squeeze. Her face became contorted. Her jaw set. Her veins began popping out of her forehead. Her glasses fell off her face. Her entire body shook back and forth from her intense struggle with the lemon as she squeezed it with all her might.

BOOM!!

Out popped one drop of lemon juice!!!

The audience erupted in applause! The sounds of clapping, whistles and cheers rang throughout the fair. The strongman was blown away as he was compelled to show the audience the plate on which the drop of lemon juice had fallen. The old lady stood there onstage with her hands on her knees as she collected her breath. It was a scene to behold.

Then the strongman walked over with a check he had just written out for $1,000 and handed it to the lady as he said: "Ma'am, you have got to tell us. I've never had anyone squeeze an extra drop of juice out of that lemon How did you do it?"

She replied: "Sir, I have to tell you. I am 74 years old. I just lost my husband. I've got three grandchildren that we're raising and I just lost my job. I needed that money."

The old lady was inspired. She was motivated. She had a reason WHY she needed to squeeze that juice out of the lemon. **With a big enough reason why, you will always find a way how.**

Your reason why is the fuel that burns the fire of inspiration and motivation inside of you.

So what is your "why"? Why do you do what you do? Why are you reading this right now? What do you want to accomplish in your life, this season, this week, today? What is your process for making those dreams a reality?

Most people think inspiration and motivation are things that you can do once in a while by reading a book, watching a movie or hearing a motivational speaker. Most people think that is all it takes for you to stay motivated. Realistically, that could not be farther from the truth. Although those experiences may spark a flame, in order to fan the flame and make it burn with a passion, you must have a BIG reason why.

> "It's not the job of other people to make my life euphoric; it's up to me."
>
> **Wayne Chrebet**
> **Former NFL wide receiver**

MOTIVATION IS A DAILY DECISION

Imagine only brushing your teeth once a week. I hope, for everyone's sake, that you are disgusted by the thought of brushing your teeth only once a week! Your teeth would become yellow, feel hairy and would develop cavities and/or rot. In addition, nobody would want to hold a conversation with you because your breath would blow them away. My point is that you cannot brush your teeth once a week or take a bath once a week and expect your teeth to look good or you to smell good.

Inspiration and motivation work the same way as dental hygiene, except they are not for your oral health but for your mental performance health. You should mentally absorb some form of inspiration daily to motivate you in your preparation and performance. Do not read something inspiring once a week. Do not motivate yourself or your team once or even a couple times a week. Inspiration and motivation must be performed every single day.

THE DAILY DOMINATOR & FOOTBALL

This is why I wrote the book *The Daily Dominator*. With The DOMINATOR you get to read one page a day of mental conditioning material so that you can do a little a lot, not a lot a little, and maximize your football mental game. Having everyone in your program read the same page each day and then breaking it down at practice or in your positional meetings takes the guesswork out of having to create your own mental conditioning program. Your "do a little a lot" each day is already done; you just have to break it down with your team.

ADVERTISE TO YOURSELF

Have you ever wondered why companies are willing to pay three million dollars for a thirty-second commercial during the Super Bowl? The common response to this question is that tens of millions of people watch the Super Bowl. This is true, but the real reason that advertising works is that advertisements create lasting images within the mind, so that when people go out to consume products, those products from the advertisements jump to the front of their minds.

The same tactics of advertising apply to inspiring peak performance. Advertising to yourself will enhance your preparation and competition by inspiring your performance. Similar to any marketing consultant, before creating sporadic marketing pitches you must know what message or product you are trying to advertise and the most effective methods for marketing that product.

With mental conditioning, the product is the mindset of a peak performer and how that mindset leads to your football success. Advertising to yourself through various strategies will help you to create the peak performance mentality you desire and help you to win more games on the gridiron.

KEVIN YOUNG – OLYMPIC ADVERTISING

The current world record holder in the 400-meter hurdles, with a time of 46.78 seconds, is the 1992 Summer Olympics gold medalist Kevin Young. When Young got to the Olympic Village in Barcelona, he advertised his Olympic goal to himself by writing it down, everywhere. When asked about his preparation in an interview after his world record performance, Young responded by saying: "My goal this year was to run 46.89. I wrote that everywhere in my room, even here up at the Village. I took a pencil and wrote it all on the wall. I integrated it into a lot of things I do at home. I just got into the habit of writing the number around, everywhere I go."

Young used the power of self-advertising his goals by putting his goal in writing, where he could see it often for motivation. As an aspiring peak performer, you too should advertise your goals to yourself by putting them everywhere you can see them. If you truly desire something, you should be able to visualize it as you go through your day at every turn. Self-advertising helps you to focus on what you want, not what you are trying to avoid.

CAIN'S CHALK TALK:
What goals can you write out and post around your room?

_____

_____

SIGNS OF SUCCESS

An excellent habit to develop is collecting inspirational phrases, pictures and images to create "signs of success" to hang around your living space. This provides you with visuals for motivation that you will see on a daily basis. When you see these signs of success every day, it becomes a part of your everyday thought process. After a few days or a week seeing a particular sign, your goal will be to commit this sign of success to memory and, more importantly, to have it effectively motivate you to action.

Players most often self-advertise signs of success by hanging photos, quotes and other images all around their bedroom and locker. Pictures of athletes or coaches who inspire them, quotes that motivate them to continuously check in on their perspective, and mental conditioning statements such as ***Don't count the days, make the days count"*** are reminders of the importance of today. Whenever you need them, these inspirational advertisements catch your eye and keep you inspired and motivated on your journey up The Mountain of Excellence.

The signs of success are simple ways to advertise the peak performance mentality and mental conditioning principles you want to adopt in sport and life.

MAKE YOUR OWN SIGNS OF SUCCESS

Draw from the material and information you have acquired from this book and make your own signs of success. By creating your signs of success, you put your knowledge of peak performance to use and enhance the process of mentally conditioning the habit of excellence.

CAIN'S CHALK TALK:
Based on the content within this manual, what are three captions for signs of success that you will hang in your room to stay inspired?

_____

_____

_____

EXAMPLES OF SELF-ADVERTISEMENT

Now that you know the importance of the signs of success and have created mental game marketing campaigns for yourself, let me share with you what other players have reported hanging in their rooms as signs of success. Remember, at all levels of competition, you are never too young, too old, too bad or too good to stay inspired.

1. A vision board collage of all your goals and what you want to accomplish.

2. A picture of your national or state championship stadium where that event will be held.

3. A poster of Muhammad Ali or other athletes who inspire the mentality that you want to develop.

4. A poster of The Miracle On Ice or other great moments in sport that motivate you to do the work it takes so that you too may experience a similar great moment.

5. An inspirational quote from your favorite piece of literature.

BATHROOM MIRROR – DRY ERASE MARKER

Another great technique worth revisiting so you can stay inspired is to write your goals on your bathroom mirror with a dry erase marker. Whenever you enter the bathroom, you will see your goals and be reminded of the mindset you want to develop to become a peak performer. Essentially, your mirror becomes a goal-oriented sign of success.

I have worked with professional mixed martial arts fighters who, immediately upon arriving in Vegas at their hotel room, take out a dry erase marker and write their mental game reminders on the mirror. Writing on their mirror sets the tone for their peak performance mentality; whenever they enter the bathroom, they are reminded of their desired mindset and the need to focus on that mindset and process for performance excellence.

GOAL CARDS CARRIED ALL THE TIME

Another strategy you can use is to carry a card in your wallet with your personal goals displayed on it. Carrying a goal card will make you 35% more likely to make those goals come true because you have constant reinforcement whenever you open your wallet. Whenever you do open your wallet, take a look at that card and mentally check in with how you are moving forward to achieve your goals. This form of self-advertising will go wherever you go.

ATHLETIC TAPE & WRIST BAND ADVERTISING

During preparation or in competition, a great method of self-advertising is to write inspirational messages on athletic tape or wrist clothing. Wrist tape and wrist bands are effective places for self-advertising because you constantly see the messages in front of yourself. Many football players will write their goals on their wrist tape so they are reminded of what they must work on or are trying to accomplish.

VISION BOARDS

One of the best motivational exercises you can do as an individual and as a team to help with inspiration and motivation is to create a vision board. A vision board is simply a collage of your goals and what you desire to accomplish. I strongly encourage you to create a vision board for yourself, and if you are on a team, I highly recommend you create one together as a team-building and team-focusing exercise.

You will never outperform your self-image. Making a vision board of images will inspire you to accomplish your goals. Place it where you will see it every day. This will keep your goals in the front of your mind and motivate you to achieve them. I personally started using vision boards in 2007 and annually revisit my own board the first week in July. Below is a picture of my personal vision board.

As you can see on my vision board, I want to speak in every state in the country. The ones that are white are the ones where I have not had a chance to speak YET. I want to help teams win national championships (accomplished in 2012). I want to spend more time fishing and hiking in the mountains of Vermont. I want to read at least one book every month. I want to be a better listener. I want to keep my weight under 200 pounds (198lbs at present). I want to have better balance in my life between work and relaxation, and I want to live the core values of being positive, disciplined, progressive and committed to others. I also wanted to be a #1 Best-selling Author (which has been accomplished with my first book *Toilets, Bricks, Fish Hooks and PRIDE*).

I keep my vision board with me in my binder and I look at it multiple times each week. I have a copy of my vision board on my desk at home and on my desk at the office. The vision board serves as a reminder for me to constantly ask myself: *Is what I am working on right now helping me get to where I want to go?* The vision board is great for helping create the awareness you need to constantly check in on your progress towards achieving your goals and to refocus you on what you want to accomplish.

WORK TO MAKE "IT" WORK

Here's the significant difference between peak performers and the rest of humanity: Peak performers understand that you must work to make "it" work. Whatever that "it" is, it's all about investing time and energy into a process of development that will make you excellent at what you do, and thus will bring you success. The vision board process has worked for me, it has worked for Jack Canfield (author of *Chicken Soup for the Soul*), and it has worked for thousands of other people.

WATCH OUT FOR THE NEGAHOLICS

If you are an unenthusiastic, pessimistic cynic, often referred to as a "Debbie Downer" or a negaholic, and you believe that ***"This mental conditioning stuff is bogus, I just want to play"*** or ***"This stuff is never actually going to improve my performance,"*** well, you are right!

Whether you think you can or think you can't, you are right!

Since you have made it this far in the manual, it is clear you are not one of these people. My hope is that, based on all the previous lessons learned in mental conditioning, you can see it is quite apparent this imaginary skeptic obviously has zero knowledge about how peak performance and mental conditioning apply to the journey of excellence in the game of football.

What real-life skeptics do not understand is that ***you have to work to make it work.*** The reason mental conditioning exercises will not work for them is a result of their refusal to try and make it work. It is not rocket science - if you do not attempt to make something work, of course it will not! It is the same logic as the old saying, "You miss 100 percent of the shots you do not take." You must believe in the benefits of mental conditioning for your performance to improve, and there are real, tangible payoffs.

The use of signs of success and vision boards will help you stay focused on your goals, and they will help you to get motivated and stay inspired to DO THE WORK that it takes to be successful.

CAIN'S COACHING POINT:
If you noticed anyone on your team who has openly dismissed mental conditioning and stopped reading this book, reflect on how his attitude and actions affect the team. If his mentality is adversely affecting team chemistry, I'd suggest confronting that teammate or making your coach aware of the situation as an expression of genuine concern for the well-being of the team throughout the season. Sometimes these moments can make all the difference in an athlete's career or even the person's life, because someone took the time and cared enough to step up, maybe more than that person cares about himself.

MOTIVATIONAL MOTION PICTURES

Motivational videos, inspirational movies, and highlight reels are another tremendous tool for peak performers. Similar to the video enhancement in mental imagery, there is no debating that watching some form of motivational motion picture or video before a practice or a game will inspire your performance on that day.

Watching a personal motivational video clip every morning as part of your morning routine also provides great reinforcement for the kind of person and player you want to be today. Regardless of how you feel when you wake up, the video clips you watch will get you fired up to DOMINATE that day and do the work necessary to advance further up The Mountain of Excellence.

CAIN'S CHALK TALK:
I challenge you to make your own personal highlight video. You can use footage of yourself or of others on YouTube to inspire your performance. Then watch this video on a routine basis.

INSPIRE YOUR DAILY DOMINATION

Whether you read a chapter in this book, watch an inspirational movie clip or use any number of the various methods for inspirational motivation, you must build motivation into your daily routine to become inspired to take action. You will have more success spending 3-5 minutes a day getting inspired and motivated than you will if you spend one hour once a week. Remember, if you get inspired a little a lot, you will have more success than if you get inspired a lot a little.

By the end of using this book, you will possess the information necessary to transform yourself into a peak performing football player. It is thus imperative that you motivate yourself to master the mental game in your daily preparation and performance ACTION, not just understand what you should do. Be the one who DOES IT!

Remember, intelligence is acting on the knowledge you have acquired. Use the strategies for motivation and inspiration from within this chapter to inspire your climb up to the summit of The Mountain of Excellence.

CHAPTER #10 REVIEW

☐ Have a big reason "why" and you will always find a way how.

☐ Make yourself inspired daily by reviewing motivational material.

☐ Advertise your goals to yourself.

☐ Make signs of success for motivation.

☐ Write daily goals on your mirror and make longer-term goal cards.

☐ Self-advertise during performance by writing on athletic tape.

☐ Create vision boards for performance goals.

☐ Work to make your goals a reality.

☐ Watch motivational video clips for inspiration.

☐ If you get inspired a little a lot, you will have more success than if you get inspired a lot a little.

CONCLUSION

PERFORMANCE EXCELLENCE

> "There was a very negative culture. They had a loser's mentality. The first thing you had to do was change the attitude, which is very hard to do. You have to find out what the source of it is, get rid of the players who cause the defeatist undertow, get a lot of new players, and get them to put out their best.'"
>
> ***Bill Belichick***
> ***Head Football Coach***
> ***New England Patriots***

Excellence is being at your best when it means the most – every single day and every single play.

This concept rules supreme in peak performance, transcending and penetrating all other aspects of mental conditioning. It is assuming personal responsibility in your daily pursuit of excellence that will make you a champion, because consistency of effort wins. Excellence is about the cultivation of superior mental strength through the process of establishing the proper routines, positive self-talk and a champion's mentality in preparation for inevitable battles through adversity in the game and in life.

After all the mental conditioning material we have covered in this book, you should be both informed and well on your way to achieving your goal of performance excellence in football. We have outlined the fundamental principles of mental conditioning and discussed how to adapt these principles and apply them on your journey to the summit of The Mountain of Football Excellence. This conclusion explains the purpose of necessary devotion to excellence within performance.

EXCELLENCE IS A LIFESTYLE, NOT AN EVENT

Truly excellent individuals recognize that excellence is not something you do once in a while; you must strive to be excellent all the time - that is, twenty-four hours a day, seven days a week, and three hundred sixty-five days a year. Excellence is a stain you can't wipe off. I hope this book has stained you with excellence.

THREE DOORS & THE LAW OF AVERAGES

You have three doors you can choose to open. You can open the door called WIN, you can open the door called LOSE, or you can open the door called EXCELLENCE. The pursuit of excellence is about more than winning; performance excellence transcends winning. Excellence is a lifestyle; winning is an event that takes place at a moment in time.

Remember that the law of averages says that if you play your best, you give yourself the best chance to win, but you are not guaranteed to win. As a peak performer, you cannot control the outcome; all you can do is work the process to the best of your ability and give yourself the best opportunity for performance success on that day and on that play. The daily pursuit of excellence is the only way to get there.

THE EXCELLENCE OF BLUE ANGELS

Excellence is about preparing more than other people are willing to and working smarter than other people think is necessary. It is paying close attention to detail within the process in order to give you the results you desire. The Blue Angels are a group of United States Navy Fighter Pilots that perform aerial shows all over the country. What their audiences witness is excellence in motion. What the audience does not see is that the entire performance process demands precision and a commitment to excellence before, and after, they take to the skies.

As some of the most dedicated and excellent performers on the planet, the Blue Angels use mental imagery, video analysis, and a routine brief and debriefing process. Each of these takes about twice as long as the flight itself to prepare for and then learn from each event they perform. The Blue Angels are known for their tight diamond formation in the air, where only 36 inches (just one yard!) separate a plane from its wingtip to the canopy of the other planes (36 inches is about how far your head is from your feet when you sit down and read this). They perform aerial maneuvers at a speed of one mile every 9 seconds or a closure rate, two planes flying directly towards each other at one mile every 4-½ seconds - almost 1,000 miles per hour. There is no room for error, and team excellence in their performance is critical.

PURSUIT OF EXCELLENCE OVER PERFECTION

The Blue Angels understand that their pursuit of excellence is different than the pursuit of perfection. They know that there has never been the perfect flight. They are constantly evaluating performance on video, looking for areas of improvement, paying close attention to the details of their flights, and even evaluating the way they march to their airplanes. The Blue Angels team is a model of excellence, and these pilots are truly dedicated to progress and making the team better in their pursuit of excellence TODAY!

When you see the Blue Angels or other peak performers like Darrelle Revis, Peyton Manning or Ray Lewis, they make what they do look very easy and we think they are gifted. Do not be fooled by their grace and proficient performance. Although they may have been blessed with a few faster twitch muscle fibers than Joe Normal, even they have climbed The Mountain of Excellence one step at a time, and they would be the first to tell you so.

A WORLD CHAMPION STATE OF MIND

Whether you have the physical talent of a world champion or not is irrelevant. Physical skill makes these champions visibly impressive, but more important is their mental toughness. The story behind their physical prowess is the story of their mental prowess - because it is their incredible work ethic, their capacity to embrace adversity, and their insatiable desire to improve to which they owe their success. One of the most beautiful aspects of the mental game is that, regardless of physical skill, you can become a master of the mental game.

Most people believe that you must be great before you can practice like the great ones. Well, most people have got it all wrong. Anyone can execute this program to cultivate the mindset of a champion. You may not lift the same amount of weight or run the same distance, but anyone can prepare and practice with the same mental intensity of a world champion. All physical performance programs should necessarily be tailored to the physical capabilities of the individual, but mental performance programs may be adopted universally. The fundamentals of mental conditioning may be practiced by anyone willing to actively pursue the summit of The Mountain of Excellence.

THE CLIMB IS THE DISCOVERY

As we have discussed throughout this manual, performance, in sport and in life, is comparable to that of a journey up a mountain. The journey is yours and you alone have the ability to set the tone of your performance to conquer the climb. The mountain you set your sights on is your choice and the journey is your discovery.

Each mountain you approach will require different physical skills that you must master, but the mental skill will remain the same. There will be some mountains that serve as pleasure climbs, while others will challenge your very existence by demanding every ounce of your physical and mental abilities. Sometimes you will be climbing a mountain and you will realize you no longer wish to reach the summit. Sometimes you will need to return to base camp, take a break and return to conquer the summit at a later date. Each journey up a mountain is a journey of self-discovery, and through each experience you learn a little about yourself and you learn a little bit about the journey. At the end of the day, it is the journey to the summit, not the summit itself, that makes reaching the summit worthwhile.

THE JOURNEY IS THE REWARD,
THE DESTINATION IS THE DISEASE

My hope is that by the end of this book you will have learned how to be an independent, peak performance mountaineer on the football field and in life – one who understands that although you may reach the summit of the mountain you are climbing, there is no summit in life and there is no summit to your excellence.

You are on a journey in which the journey is the reward and the destination is the disease. You must understand that every climb is a process and that proper preparation is imperative. You must create a mental road map, detailing where you want to go and who you must become to be worthy of reaching the summit. Remember, if you want more, you must become more.

Becoming more will give you the best chance to reach the summit of any mountain. Once you reach the summit and have thoroughly enjoyed the view, it is time to return to base camp and start climbing another.

CAIN'S COACHING POINT:
There will always be another mountain to climb. Throughout your journeys up the Mountains of Excellence, recognize there is no final summit; there is no finish line. You are on a journey called life and your best bet is to DOMINATE THE DAY, every day, and enjoy this amazing ride.

SUCCESS = THE RESULT OF EXCELLENCE

I have said this before, and I will repeat myself for emphasis. There is no shortcut to performance excellence; there is no easy way to the summit of your mountain. *You don't get the same satisfaction of helicoptering to the summit as you do from climbing.*

Excellence is something you cannot purchase or be gifted, just as success is not something you simply randomly discover. Excellence is the result of a self-transformative journey to becoming more. A journey that you choose to actively endure, and once you develop a strict adherence to personal excellence, you are bound to discover the success you are looking for in *ALL ASPECTS OF YOUR LIFE!*

CAIN'S COACHING POINT:
If you have found value in using this book and if it has helped you in any way, consider giving a copy to five people whom you care about and want to see take their performance to the next level. By giving this book to others, you are helping them find the ideas and mental keys that will unlock their potential. You will help them live a more fulfilled and excellent journey as they climb their Mountain of Excellence. This manual could forever alter the course of someone's life. It could be you who provides the push as a great teammate. Without you, they might never even start hiking.

Write down five people to whom you will give a copy of this manual:

1) _____

2) _____

3) _____

4) _____

5) _____

THE MENTAL CONDITIONS FOR EXCELLENCE

Through this book you have learned many mental conditioning strategies and peak performance principles to help you proceed on your journey to the summit of The Mountain of Excellence. Regardless of your sport or profession, the utilization of these mental conditioning principles and fundamentals are necessary to help achieve an elite and excellent performance state of mind.

At the conclusion of going through The Mental Game of Football, you have learned how to:

• Live in the present moment and maximize your time

• Act differently than how you feel and start having good bad days

• Focus on the process over the outcome

• Identify what you can control and what you cannot

• Have your own personal philosophy and core values for life

• Challenge your limiting beliefs and your perspective

• Stay positive in the face of adversity

• Develop preparation and performance routines for a consistently high-level performance

• Take responsibility for your performance and life

• Relax, recover and gain control of your thoughts, feelings and emotions

• Recognize your signal lights and develop the awareness to win

• Release negative thoughts and refocus back to the present when you get distracted

• Move from intelligence and thinking to action and results

• Use mental imagery to help you prepare and be more confident in your performance

• Inspire and motivate yourself to make the impossible possible

• Take action steps to make excellence a lifestyle, not an event

Remember, you will reach the summit of The Mountain of Excellence by focusing on the next 30 feet. When you take Personal Responsibility In Daily Excellence, everything else will take care of itself. Today, sign your name with excellence on everything and everyone you touch, and I will see you at the summit!

_____

YOUR SIGNATURE HERE   DATE

In Excellence,
Your Mental Conditioning Coach

Brian M. Cain
@BrianCainPeak, www.BrianCain.com

CONCLUSION REVIEW

☐ Excellence is being at your best when it means the most – every single day.

☐ Excellence is a lifestyle, not an event.

☐ You have three doors you can choose to open. You can open the door called WIN, you can open the door called LOSE, or you can open the door called EXCELLENCE.

☐ Excellence is about preparing more than other people are willing to, and working smarter than other people think is necessary.

☐ The pursuit of excellence is constructive; the pursuit of perfection will destroy you.

☐ Anyone can develop a world champion state of mind.

☐ The journey makes reaching the summit worthwhile.

☐ The journey is the reward and the destination is the disease.

☐ Success is the result of excellence.

☐ When you take PRIDE (Personal Responsibility In Daily Excellence) in your performance, everything else will take care of itself.

DOMINATE THE DAY!

ABOUT THE AUTHOR

WHO IS BRIAN M. CAIN?

Brian M. Cain, MS, CMAA, is a #1 best-selling author, speaker, trainer and expert in the fields of Mental Conditioning and Peak Performance for football.

He has worked with coaches, athletes and teams at the Olympic level and in the National Football League (NFL), National Basketball Association (NBA), National Hockey League (NHL), Ultimate Fighting Championship (UFC), and Major League Baseball (MLB) and with top high school and college football programs in the nation.

Cain has also worked with athletic teams in some of the top college athletic departments around the country including the University of Alabama, Auburn University, Florida State University, the University of Iowa, the University of Maryland, the University of Mississippi, Mississippi State University, Oregon State University, the University of Southern California, the University of Tennessee, Vanderbilt University, Washington State University, Yale University, Texas A & M, TCU, Baylor, the University of Georgia, the University of North Carolina, Notre Dame, and many others.

Cain has worked as a mental conditioning consultant with numerous high school, state and national championship programs. He has delivered his award-winning seminars and presentations at coaches' clinics, leadership summits and athletic directors' conventions all over the country. As a high school athletic director, he is one of the youngest ever to receive the Certified Master Athletic Administration Certification from the National Interscholastic Athletic Administrators Association.

A highly sought-after Peak Performance Coach, clinician, and keynote and motivational speaker, Cain delivers his message with

www.BrianCain.com

passion and enthusiasm, in an engaging style that keeps his audiences energized while being educated. As someone who lives what he teaches, Cain will inspire you and give you the tools necessary to get the most out of your career.

Cain lives in Southlake, Texas and is avialble to work with your staff and players on implementing a mental conditioning and peak performance program specific for your goals. He also works 1-1 with many of the top players in the nation on helping them develop the mental toughness, leadership and winning mindset it takes to succeed at the next level.

Please visit www.briancain.com/monday to sign up for his weekly newsletter. Also, visit www.briancain.com/calendar to see when Cain will be in your area so you can experience the benefits of having him come in and work with your team.

ABOUT THE CO-AUTHOR

WHO IS DANIEL C. NOLAN?

Dan Nolan is a nationally renowned expert on teaching core values, sportsmanship and peak performance skills coaches and athletes can use.

Dan teaches audiences how to obtain better results on and off the field with simple-to-use and effective strategies to turbocharge performance. Nolan is also a high school educator and football coach in Vermont and was named the 2008 Coach of the Year.

Nolan has worked with top college and high school teams around the country and was a featured speaker at the 2009 Massachusetts Interscholastic Athletic Association Sportsmanship Summit, the 2012 Vermont Coaches School, the 2012 Northwest Independent School District (Dallas, TX) Coaches School, and the Ellensburg (WA) Football Camp. Nolan will engage your group with a fast-paced, audience-participation-filled event where you will take a look inside of yourself and find out just how good you can be.

Using a multidisciplinary approach, Dan helps coaches, athletes and organizations develop their competitive edge. Please visit coachnolan.net to sign up for his free book of leadership anecdotes.

ADDITIONAL RESOURCES

HOW YOU CAN CONTINUE TO BECOME A MASTER OF THE MENTAL GAME

Cain offers a range of training materials to get you and your team to the top of your game.

Available at www.BrianCain.com

MASTERS OF THE MENTAL GAME SERIES BOOKS MENTAL CONDITIONING RESOURCES

Champions Tell All:
Inexpensive Experience From The World's Best

Cain provides you with all access to some of the World's greatest performers. Learn from mixed martial arts world champions and college All-Americans about mental toughness.

The Daily Dominator:
Perform Your Best Today. Every Day!

You get 366 Daily Mental Conditioning lessons to help you start your day down the path to excellence. Investing time each day with Cain is your best way to become your best self.

The Mental Conditioning Manual:
Your Blueprint For Excellence

This is the exact system Cain uses to build champions and masters of the mental game. It has helped produce NCAA and High School, champions, MMA world champions, and more.

So What, Next Pitch!
How To Play Your Best When It Means The Most
A compilation of interviews with top coaches and players where Cain teaches you their systems and tricks. Learn from the insights of these masters of the mental game.

Toilets, Bricks, Fish Hooks and PRIDE:
The Peak Performance Toolbox EXPOSED
Go inside the most successful programs in the country that use Cain's Peak Performance System. Use this book to unlock your potential and learn to play your best when it means the most.

The Peak Performance System (P.R.I.D.E.)
Personal Responsibility In Daily Excellence
This big, video-based training program is Cain's signature training program for coaches, athletes and teams. It will take you step by step to the top of the performance mountain.

Diamond Domination Training:
The New 4RIP3 System for Baseball and Softball
This training program is being used by 11 teams in the NCAA top 25 in college baseball and 8 of the top 25 in college softball. It will help you and your team to unlock your potential and play the best baseball and softball of your life.

4RIP3 MMA Mental Conditioning System
Get the techniques used by the best fighters in the world and start bringing the fighter you are in the gym into the cage. It will help you unlock your potential, teach you drills to sharpen your focus and give you the confidence of a champion.

And more at www.BrianCain.com

"

CONNECT WITH CAIN

YOUR LINK TO DOING A LITTLE A LOT, NOT A LOT A LITTLE

 www.twitter.com/briancainpeak

 www.facebook.com/briancainpeak

 www.linkedin.com/briancainpeak

 www.youtube.com/wwwbriancaincom

 www.briancain.com/itunes

SIGN UP FOR BRIAN CAIN'S
MONDAY MENTAL CONDITIONING MESSAGE

Cain's Monday Message is full of information to help you unlock your potential and perform at your best when it means the most. Subscribe for FREE and get a bonus audio training. www.BrianCain.com/Monday

CONCENTRATION GRIDS

ONE NUMBER/PLAY AT A TIME

Brian Cain Peak Performance, LLC
Concentration Training Grid
www.BrianCain.com

86	54	04	72	20	05	34	79	52	17
73	43	50	70	44	12	28	59	94	35
45	62	63	97	51	95	91	67	84	75
27	69	23	00	08	83	09	41	65	78
80	39	68	47	29	93	36	30	38	42
61	53	19	48	49	74	40	18	15	21
60	01	14	22	64	07	58	02	32	16
13	31	26	71	66	33	06	85	10	89
76	46	98	37	99	24	57	11	55	82
92	25	81	96	87	88	77	03	56	90

Brian Cain Peak Performance, LLC
Concentration Training Grid
www.BrianCain.com

86	54	04	72	20	05	34	79	52	17
73	43	50	70	44	12	28	59	94	35
45	62	63	97	51	95	91	67	84	75
27	69	23	00	08	83	09	41	65	78
80	39	68	47	29	93	36	30	38	42
61	53	19	48	49	74	40	18	15	21
60	01	14	22	64	07	58	02	32	16
13	31	26	71	66	33	06	85	10	89
76	46	98	37	99	24	57	11	55	82
92	25	81	96	87	88	77	03	56	90

Brian Cain Peak Performance, LLC
Concentration Training Grid
www.BrianCain.com

86	54	04	72	20	05	34	79	52	17
73	43	50	70	44	12	28	59	94	35
45	62	63	97	51	95	91	67	84	75
27	69	23	00	08	83	09	41	65	78
80	39	68	47	29	93	36	30	38	42
61	53	19	48	49	74	40	18	15	21
60	01	14	22	64	07	58	02	32	16
13	31	26	71	66	33	06	85	10	89
76	46	98	37	99	24	57	11	55	82
92	25	81	96	87	88	77	03	56	90

Brian Cain Peak Performance, LLC
Concentration Training Grid
www.BrianCain.com

86	54	04	72	20	05	34	79	52	17
73	43	50	70	44	12	28	59	94	35
45	62	63	97	51	95	91	67	84	75
27	69	23	00	08	83	09	41	65	78
80	39	68	47	29	93	36	30	38	42
61	53	19	48	49	74	40	18	15	21
60	01	14	22	64	07	58	02	32	16
13	31	26	71	66	33	06	85	10	89
76	46	98	37	99	24	57	11	55	82
92	25	81	96	87	88	77	03	56	90

Brian Cain Peak Performance, LLC
Concentration Training Grid
www.BrianCain.com

86	54	04	72	20	05	34	79	52	17
73	43	50	70	44	12	28	59	94	35
45	62	63	97	51	95	91	67	84	75
27	69	23	00	08	83	09	41	65	78
80	39	68	47	29	93	36	30	38	42
61	53	19	48	49	74	40	18	15	21
60	01	14	22	64	07	58	02	32	16
13	31	26	71	66	33	06	85	10	89
76	46	98	37	99	24	57	11	55	82
92	25	81	96	87	88	77	03	56	90

Brian Cain Peak Performance, LLC
Concentration Training Grid
www.BrianCain.com

86	54	04	72	20	05	34	79	52	17
73	43	50	70	44	12	28	59	94	35
45	62	63	97	51	95	91	67	84	75
27	69	23	00	08	83	09	41	65	78
80	39	68	47	29	93	36	30	38	42
61	53	19	48	49	74	40	18	15	21
60	01	14	22	64	07	58	02	32	16
13	31	26	71	66	33	06	85	10	89
76	46	98	37	99	24	57	11	55	82
92	25	81	96	87	88	77	03	56	90

Brian Cain Peak Performance, LLC
Concentration Training Grid
www.BrianCain.com

86	54	04	72	20	05	34	79	52	17
73	43	50	70	44	12	28	59	94	35
45	62	63	97	51	95	91	67	84	75
27	69	23	00	08	83	09	41	65	78
80	39	68	47	29	93	36	30	38	42
61	53	19	48	49	74	40	18	15	21
60	01	14	22	64	07	58	02	32	16
13	31	26	71	66	33	06	85	10	89
76	46	98	37	99	24	57	11	55	82
92	25	81	96	87	88	77	03	56	90

Brian Cain Peak Performance, LLC
Concentration Training Grid
www.BrianCain.com

86	54	04	72	20	05	34	79	52	17
73	43	50	70	44	12	28	59	94	35
45	62	63	97	51	95	91	67	84	75
27	69	23	00	08	83	09	41	65	78
80	39	68	47	29	93	36	30	38	42
61	53	19	48	49	74	40	18	15	21
60	01	14	22	64	07	58	02	32	16
13	31	26	71	66	33	06	85	10	89
76	46	98	37	99	24	57	11	55	82
92	25	81	96	87	88	77	03	56	90

Brian Cain Peak Performance, LLC
Concentration Training Grid
www.BrianCain.com

86	54	04	72	20	05	34	79	52	17
73	43	50	70	44	12	28	59	94	35
45	62	63	97	51	95	91	67	84	75
27	69	23	00	08	83	09	41	65	78
80	39	68	47	29	93	36	30	38	42
61	53	19	48	49	74	40	18	15	21
60	01	14	22	64	07	58	02	32	16
13	31	26	71	66	33	06	85	10	89
76	46	98	37	99	24	57	11	55	82
92	25	81	96	87	88	77	03	56	90

Brian Cain Peak Performance, LLC
Concentration Training Grid
www.BrianCain.com

86	54	04	72	20	05	34	79	52	17
73	43	50	70	44	12	28	59	94	35
45	62	63	97	51	95	91	67	84	75
27	69	23	00	08	83	09	41	65	78
80	39	68	47	29	93	36	30	38	42
61	53	19	48	49	74	40	18	15	21
60	01	14	22	64	07	58	02	32	16
13	31	26	71	66	33	06	85	10	89
76	46	98	37	99	24	57	11	55	82
92	25	81	96	87	88	77	03	56	90

NOTES PAGES
KEEPING IT ALL IN ONE PLACE

_____

_____

_____

_____

_____

_____

_____

_____

_____

_____

_____

_____

_____

_____

_____

_____

_____

_____

www.BrianCain.com